A Family of Poets:
The Legacy of Birdell and Elva Sorensen

A Family of Poets:
The Legacy of Elva and Birdell Sorensen

Family Poetry

With story or emotion,
With tall tale or song,
Poets speak of life and living,
In this world where we belong.

Jack London with his tales,
Of the treacherous frozen north,
Tennyson whose heroes,
Help us see what life is worth.

Dickenson and Wordsworth,
Sharing beauty that they see,
In nature, in humankind,
Sets our spirits free.

Some use verse to free or soothe,
An aching soul or broken heart,
To give release from slaving pain,
To find a way to a new start

Whether joy or pain or fear,
To poke some fun or question why,
To make a point or praise the Lord,
To give a laugh or breathe a sigh;

Paper marked by thoughtful pen,
The heartfelt verse, the crafted
word;
No better way to speak the heart,
No better way that thoughts are
heard.

So when we gather here today,
To share our thoughts with those
we love,

We share a stage with greatness,
We share an ancient trove.

Everyone who speaks today,
Everyone who reads a poem,
Is adding to our family's name,
To our story, to our tome.

My sister, my grandchild,
My nephew, my niece,
All sharing words from the heart,
Give me comfort, give me peace.

Wisdom from my mother,
Humor from my son,
My daughter reminiscing,
I love them everyone.

I put you on a pedestal,
Above Browning or Wordsworth,
Above Tennyson or Frost.
To me you all have greater worth.

Honest thoughts from a child,
Are more precious to me,
Than all the famous poets,
In all their reverie.

Let us remember what's important,
As we live our lives each day,
It's the living poem of family,
What we do and what we say.

John Sorensen, 2017

A Family of Poets

Poetry by the descendants of

Birdell and Elva Sorensen

Logos Ethos Pathos Publishing
Pittsburgh, Pennsylvania

Copyright

A Family of Poets

By the descendants of

Birdell and Elva Sorensen

Poems from the family Reunions

Stories and Poetry from our lives

Edited by:
Morgan Templar

Dedication

In Loving Memory of

Elva & Birdell Sorensen

Table of Contents

Foreword

Poetry is one of the oldest devices of communication and culture. Our history is told in ballads and songs as a method to easily retain both the events and the feelings of the time. Who hasn't sung, "I've been working on the railroad" or "She'll be coming 'round the mountain," yet have any of us really done or seen those things? Think about the child's poem, "Ring around the Rosies." We may not even realize we're teaching about the great plagues of the Middle Ages. But that imagery is in our minds.

Poetry, in spoken form, was abandoned by most during the twentieth century. In the Victorian era and into the nineteen teens, reciting poetry was entertainment and an art form. Our Grandmother Sorensen, who passed away in the early nineteen seventies, would gather us around and recite long, complicated ballads or poems. It's a tradition that stayed with our family to this day. Special occasions include bringing out the poems written for that day: "Auntie killed Rudolph" and "The Christmas Tree Topper" have been heard by five generations as we have gathered for Christmas.

This book contains a collection of poems written by members of the family for the annual reunion Poetry Night. Beginning in 2013, the Friday night before our big outdoor celebration, most of the family would gather and orally read or recite the poem written for the gathering. Most years were open format, though our reunions have been themed. The 2019 reunion was centered on a Viking theme and poems were requested to be written in Skaldic or Eddic (sagas) style, though all style of poems were read. In 2022 we asked for Haiku poems.

The Sorensen Family Reunion started out with a "Duck" theme, which included creating "duck" crafts with supplied materials and then racing them down the park's creek. We also had plastic ducks that could be "purchased" to raise the money for our annual gatherings. The first numbered duck to the net across the creak got a prize. Eventually we branched out to other themes:

- 2013 = Dinosaurs
- 2014 = Medieval Dragons and Monsters (and a Great Quest for Treasure)
- 2015 = Egyptian explorers
- 2016 = Find your family tree
- 2017 = Harry Potter
- 2018 = Going to space
- 2019 = Vikings
- 2021 = Star Wars
- 2022 = Water Park
- 2023 = Halloween

Each year included themed crafts and games, wooden swords for every kid made by John and Joshua, light sabers, 2-liter bottle water rockets – decorated of course, snakes, dragons, aliens and Vikings all had to be battled to get the great grand prize. And, of course, the giant pinata.

The reunion is always fun, but the Friday night poetry gathering is special. Not only does it hold excitement for the upcoming Saturday activities, but it holds an almost reverent air of bonding as a family and appreciating each other.

The poems are read aloud by the author. Prizes have been awarded in the under 12, 12-18, and 18+ age groups. This oral and written tradition is a reflection of our family, its diversity, and open acceptance of every belief and stage of life.

The poetry reading on Friday night was initially held at the home of our niece, Shannon Millet. Shannon suffered from a variety of physical disabilities, the most commonly known being Muscular Dystrophy. In spite of that, she loved having the family visit and many years her parents and brothers brought her to the reunion in her wheelchair, including bringing suction equipment for her tracheostomy to keep her breathing. Shannon passed away in 2018 and the poetry reading moved back to grandma's house.

Our father, Birdell Sorensen, passed away in 2006 before we started the annual poetry tradition. He would have loved it. Dad always had a poem to share and often recited for us. His favorite poem was *"Little Orphant Annie"* by James Whitcomb Riley. (Perhaps I'm prejudiced here as he often called me Annie, my middle name being Anne.) Our books of poetry printed in the 1950's were worn until the covers fell off. Before he passed, I recall many Sunday afternoons talking about books, poetry, science, technology, politics, religion or whatever topic was interesting as a family. Then mom (Elva) would get out her accordion and play the songs/poems of the thirties to fifties, sometimes singing along and other times just dad and the kids listening.

This love of poetry has also led several of us to be published authors and aspiring authors in a variety of genres. David Mealing, Morgan Templar, Joshua Sorensen, Lynn Sorensen, Rhea Cragun, Brian Mealing and Skye Caden have written books, poems or stories of both non-fiction and fiction, and have been published in anthologies.

Our parents raised a gifted and accomplished family. The siblings have all gone to college, some of us with advanced degrees. Not bad for a coal miner and a high school dropout who married an older man when she was 15. Our home fostered a love of learning, encouragement to be inquisitive, and a joy of coming together for games, puzzles and actual conversation.

Poetry has been at the heart of our family. This book is a collection of many of our reunion poems.

Morgan Templar
Editor, Logos, Ethos, Pathos Publishing
Pittsburgh, PA 2023

Introduction

We grew up going to family reunions.

Some of these reunions included up to eight generations from the point of origin on the family tree. We knew our cousins out to seventh cousin twice removed. I'm sure that I can't even begin to describe the logic of cousin relationship naming, but be that as it may, *we come from a very large and close-knit family.*

We had reunions on our parent's' paternal and maternal lines. And don't forget the many weddings and funerals that will still bring us together.

By the time my parents' descendants hit 50, we decided we needed a reunion for just our family. We often meet for Christmas Eve, which is another story entirely and not part of this book specifically. Grandma's birthday on the first Saturday of October is another big family gathering. But the summer reunion is different than both of those gatherings.

First of all, we limited the size. Besides our direct siblings, we invited our cousin Carrie and her parents – mom's sister Emily and Byron. Carrie's an only child and we wanted her to be included. Sometimes other cousins came, as well. We've never limited who could come.

Our reunions often have a theme. And there is Always a craft project for the kids to make something that they can then enter into the competition. Whether it is duck boats made of paper plates, balloons, and popsicle sticks or cardboard box Star Wars Pod Racers for a running race. the creativity is tapped into. It's part of our family culture.

Most years we have a raffle of items donated by the family. This is how we keep the reunion fund with some money. Usually, it raises a couple hundred dollars, and we use it for the next year's reunion. We started out asking that all raffle items be hand made to showcase everyone's skills. But as we got older and had more kids, that wasn't always practical. So, raffle items were purchased and donated. We sold tickets for a quarter, and everyone had their name in the bowl, even if they couldn't afford tickets that year. When we did the duck races, we would "rent" the plastic ducks for a dollar a duck and drop 40 or 50 ducks into the creek. It has been a good way to raise the money without pressure. We also make sure that every child has a prize for something. Nobody ever left my mother's events without some kind of gift or prize. It was just the way she was – always thinking of the kids.

Mom passed away in 2021, after the reunion. Her funeral was the week that she would have been hosting her 89th birthday party.

The Sorensen family reunion has always been creative, supporting, and full of love. Relationships built over coalitions of duck building or questing for gold in a wizard guided adventure have kept the third and fourth generation kids close.

But our Poetry is the thing that is the differentiator from other reunions. We not only write our poems, we speak them. The youngest child that can only write a one- or two-line poem to our kids with down syndrome or other disabilities all participate.

Our family is over 108 people at last count over five generations. I have included a family tree of the kids and grandkids of Elva and Birdell Sorensen. There are marriages, divorces, births and deaths. This is the core of who we are together as a family.

This book was compiled for the purpose of sharing our poetry with our family. Of course, we hope everyone that purchases it and reads it will feel the love and joy, the hope and stark realities, and the diversity of our points of view.

The Birdell and Elva Sorensen Family Tree
(Three Generations, of five as of 2023)

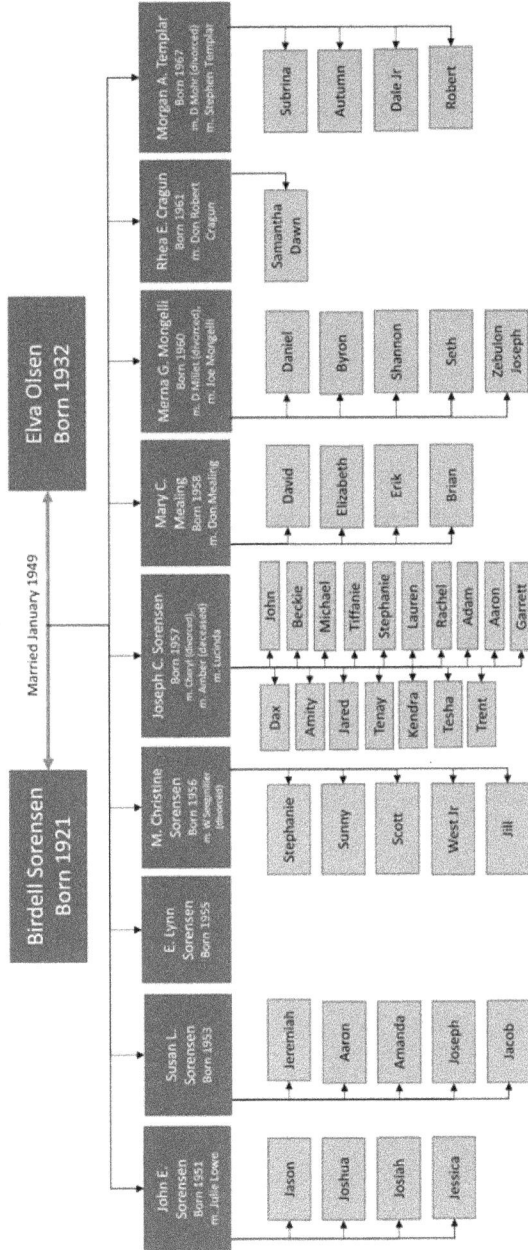

Birdell Sorensen Born 1921 — Married January 1949 — Elva Olsen Born 1932

John E. Sorensen Born 1951 m. Julie Lowe
- Jason
- Joshua
- Josiah
- Jessica

Susan L. Sorensen Born 1953
- Jeremiah
- Aaron
- Amanda
- Joseph
- Jacob

E. Lynn Sorensen Born 1955

M. Christine Sorensen Born 1956 m. W Seemster (divorced)
- Stephanie
- Sunny
- Scott
- West Jr
- Jill

Joseph C. Sorensen Born 1957 m. Cheryl (divorced), m. Amber (deceased), m. Lucinda
- John — Dax
- Beckie — Amity
- Michael — Jared
- Tiffanie — Tenay
- Stephanie — Kendra
- Lauren — Tesha
- Rachel — Trent
- Adam
- Aaron
- Garrett

Mary C. Mealing Born 1958 m. Don Mealing
- David
- Elizabeth
- Erik
- Brian

Merna G. Morgelli Born 1960 m. D Millet (divorced), m. Joe Morgelli
- Daniel
- Byron
- Shannon
- Seth
- Zebulon Joseph

Rhea E. Cragun Born 1961 m. Don Robert Cragun
- Samantha Dawn

Morgan A. Templar Born 1967 m. D Mohr (divorced) m. Stephen Templar
- Subrina
- Autumn
- Dale Jr
- Robert

Figure one: The Sorensen Family Tree

All proceeds from the sale of this book will go to the reunion fund. The following chapters are the collections from each year's poems. We didn't manage to collect everyone's poems in writing, so we're missing many of them. We'll add them in for future editions if we can gather them.

Chapter One - 2014: A Great Quest for Treasure

Heritage

We're going away?
To America you say-
Leave our families and home
For a country and faith, to roam

To England where shippers
Leave daily with loads
Put all our belongings on
Board those big white clippers

Weeks on the water
Heat hunger, sick and storms
That beat upon us asunder
Are we going to stay on top or
go under?

"Land ho!" they yell
As we run for the rail
And there she stands that girl
To welcome us from all the
world

Across grasslands and swamp
Over mountains and dell.
Heat, rain, mud and snow
Across the valleys of Hell.

At last to Utah we come
For a new life, and then some.
Scattered all over the West
To farm, build, and pass the
Test.

Now here we are once again
All together
Father, mother, sister and brother
To enjoy and love each other.

Elva Sorensen

The Bird At The Feeder

The bird at the feeder
Such a bossy thing.
Scarlet throat and rufus wing

Thirty-two ounces of sugary stuff
Des he fear there's not enough.
Or just have need to perch and glare.
Turning his head from here to there.
Watching in his greedy way
And missing the essence of the day.

What obsession to this selfish task
No other can drink from this sugar flask
Hover there you selfish being
Chitter and scold you bullying thing.
Miss the sunset, miss the sight
Of the flower blooms that grace the light.

Do I see a bit of me in you
Do I hoard the good stuff from others too.
Can I not find the will to share
To give a bit, to serve, to care.
So much time protecting my space
What more could I get from the earthly place.

Little bird
Let's open our hearts, let's fly away
Let's care less, let's enjoy the day

Let's trust that there will be enough
For me, for you, of the good sweet stuff.
Somehow someone will provide
Will fill the bottle, will take our side

Let's trust that grace
Let's cast our lot
Let's care more for what we give
And less about what we've got.

Mary Mealing

Apple Tree

An apple tree blossoms in Spring
And I love to smell the blossoms
So do the bees

Blossoms turn into delicious
apples
That are red, juicy and MINE
But I 'll share a couple with you

Sometime, if you climb
To the top of the tree
With me.

After the apples rotten it's gall
So I wait till Spring
I will smell blossoms again

Anna Bland

I Love Riding Horses

I love riding horses
They are so fast
Oh - they are so beautiful
Their tails swish in the wind
Their hooves are so shiny
And their manes are sometimes
brown
Their babies are so cute

I love riding horses
They are so fast
Oh they are beautiful
Their tails swish in the wind
Their hooves are so shiny
And their manes are brown
Horse babies are so cute

Sophia Mealing

I Love My Stuff

I love my puppies
I love my bed
I love my panda,
I love all my stuff

I love my stuffed dinosaurs
I love dinosaur Woowoo
I love my rocks
I love my rocket

I love my family
I love all my stuff

Sawyer Brimley

3

My Brain

My brain it stopped working,
It just shut off one day.
So I went to the doctor,
To see if it had shrunk away.

The doctor took his hammer,
And gave my head a thump.
It should have made a solid thud,
But it made a hollow thump.

Well, he said with some surprise,
That did not sound right.
Your head sounded hollow,
It should have sounded tight.

He listened with his stethoscope,
He said shake as fast as you can.
That sounded a little odd he said,
Like a peanut in a pan.

We had better check this out he said,
And took me to a machine.
It looked a little scary so,
I asked, What is this thing?

Don't worry said the doctor
It will not cause you pain.
It takes pictures deep inside your head,
To help me find your brain.

So stick your head inside this tube,
Close your eyes and don't move for a while.
The big machine made a lot of noise,
Thumps, whistles, groans and growls.

Then the doctor he came out,
With pictures of my head.
What is it doctor? I asked him,
Is my brain alive or dead?

I found your brain he said to me,
I think it will be alright.
It's just too loose inside your head,
It should fit in there tight.

It's bouncing all around in there,
But it should not move at all.
Your head is just too big or else,
Your brain is just too small.

Then he showed me the pictures,
And gave a puzzled shrug.
With all that bouncing in your head,
Your brain has come unplugged.

Then he reached up thru my
nose,
And put the plug in place.
And he stuffed cotton thru my
ears,
To fill the empty space.

*(At this point I start faking a
sneeze coming on – Oral cue)*

That should work he said,
As long as you don't sneeze.
What will happen then I asked,
Doctor tell me please.

You don't want to blow the
cotton out,
You know what might happen
then,
With all that empty space your
brain,
Will come unplugged again.

John Sorensen

My Dream House

From outside, looking in,
A bit old-fashioned and prosaic.
But covered porch of
Stone mosaic.

Gourmet kitchen (breakfast
nook)
Bedrooms (two or three)
And fire-placed den, each
Measuring precisely 18x33

The entry way and all the floors
Of oak or native pine (warn
gold)
Furnished "modern",
Sedate, but bold

The above described with bath
(1.5, and sauna) will surround
A stone-paved central court
(glass roofed, step-down)

This house, with all amenities,
Will be the best design
For me to fill a life-long dream;
To grow a jasmine vine.

Lynn Sorensen

Itchy Stew

A long time ago,
At a Grandma's house far away,
There was a sycamore tree
Where us grandkids always
played

It was the very best for climbing
And had a tire swing
But the glory of the sycamore
Was in a far more messy thing.

From grand imagination
Was born a masterpiece:
A plan to trick the grownups –
A concoction for them to eat.

We filled the little red wagon
With water from the hose.
Gathered round it in a circle,
Our assignments we all chose.

On GO! We scattered through
the yard
Grabbing fistfuls here and there.
We stirred it with a giant stick,
Sloshing it everywhere.

We added dirt, leaves, and twigs,
Grass and dandelion fluff,
Berries from the neighbor's
bush,
And lots of other stuff.

Then finally the itchy balls
Were dropped into the goo.
The crowning part of our
creation,
And we called it Itchy Stew.

Jessica Brimley

Picachu

Picachu, freakachu
Guess what?
Freakachu freaks out

Lucas Bland

Scary Nights

When I go to bed at night
And all the lights are out,
I sometimes lie there wide
awake,
Afraid to even shout

Hands and claws and teeth
Make scary shadows on the wall
"Oh my!" I whisper to myself,
"This isn't good at all!"

Those teeth look awfully sharp;
Those hands look awfully
strong.
I cover up my head and think,
"Those claws look awfully
long!"

I peek out of the blankets,
The moon is shining bright,
The hands and teeth and claws
Look silly in the light.

I hear the monsters making
noise,
They sound like they are roaring,
I close my eyes and go to sleep
"It's only Daddy, snoring!"

Unknown

Love

I'd waste as much daylight as I
could
Looking at you
I'll swaddle you in Love
and tell you what is true

Little boy you smile
Even when you toss and turn
The love I feel in my heart
Makes it smoulder and burn

I want you to count a million
stars
And breathe air I've never
breathed
Lucas Oak I love you
Like I never could believe

Erik Mealing

Black Friday

When November comes around
So starts the Christmas spirit
The wood stove starts to burn
So warm! We huddle near it.

But there's only just one problem
Come Turkey Day's conclusion
It's the day that comes right after
with
Concussions and contusions.

Black Friday isn't great to most
Though some pretend it's fun and
dandy
"Let's stay in line all night" they
say
"Don't be such a pansy!"

The doors they open wide
Bright and early at 6 AM
Wait! This year it's 5. No 4.
This day is such a gem!

The people they rush in
With a might l shove and push
If you don't stay on your feet
You might get squished to mush.

Now they're in the store
And the fighting really starts
Look out for that left hook!
As she scoops the shelf into her
cart.

There goes a fearsome tackle
He should be in the NFL
This place is turning out to be
Somewhere that rhymes with...bell.

The claws and fangs come out
There's blood along the floor
They want this thing and that one
Then they rush around for more.

Can more fit in here or there
E'en though the cart's o'erflowing?
Some spils along behind as
The store is finally closing.

They rush to the nearest checkout
line
The associate may lose his mind
And then the most dreadful thing
happens
Credit Card Declined

Paul Brimley

8

The Cherry Tree

I sat underneath the cherry tree,
The blossoms all covered in
dew.
I sat underneath the cherry tree,
I wish you could sit here too.

I sat underneath the cherry tree,
The birds fluttering to and fro.
I sat underneath the cherry tree,
Thinking 'bout you, ya' know.

I sat underneath the cherry tree,
No rainclouds to be seen.
I sat underneath the cherry tree,
I don't think the bees are mean.

I sat underneath the cherry tree,
Wondering what to do.
I sat underneath the cherry tree
Writing this poem for you.

Karleigh Brimley

The Shell

I was walking along the
seashore
I found a pretty shell
I didn't know if it was a snail
shell
I couldn't tell

When I got into the shower
I took the shell with me
I slipped and fell and cracked
the shell
I didn't know why

I talked to the doctors about it
The said "eat your meal"
I didn't know why
I didn't cry it was very funny

So if you're walking along the
seashore
And find a pretty shell
Don't take it into the shower
with you
Cause crack the shell and you
probably wouldn't know why

Raegan Brimley

Chapter 2 – 2015: Egyptian Explorers

Forbidden Flight

I want to soar
And feel the rush
Of doing something
Dangerous!

A forbidden flight,
Or so I'm told,
Written in
The laws of old.

A warning voice
Begs me to stay
It's tugging me
Back to the clay.

With disappointment
In my eyes
I gaze with longing
At the skies.

But then another
Whispered voice
Urges on
The outlawed choice.

It says "Take flight".
It says "Be free".
Just lift my feet
And spread my wings.

It sparks wonder
In my thoughts.
Back in the dream
My mind gets lost.

Excitement fills
My fingertips.
A daring smile
Forms on my lips.

I'll take the risk.
I'll do it nowm
And float away
Into the clouds.

Grasping hold
I take the swing,
Flying high
On Grandpa's rings.

Jessica Brimley

Fruit Cocktail

Mangos and Kiwis, Lemons
and Limes,
Bananas and Apples and
Clementines,

Strawberries and Grapes,
Plums and Cherries,
Apricots, Oranges and
Raspberries,

Papayas and Grapefruit and
Blueberries so blue,
Then mix all the fruits in a
syrupy goo.

'Cause all of these things
mixed together you see,
Make a Fruit Cocktail for you
and me.

Karleigh Brimley

Paranoid

I've always wondered
What's under my bed.
Or – what's in the closet?
Does it want me dead?
Did something creep into
My shoes overnight?
All of these thoughts
Just fill me with fright.
I wonder each moment
What lives in the shower?
I think about these
Scary things every hour.
I suspect the trash can
Contains something sinister.
And I fear for the safety
Of my little sister.
So, all of these places
I've tried to avoid.
And then people wonder
If I'm paranoid.

Skye Caden

Getting Old

It's not easy getting old,
So I've seen and been told.
But think of all the things I've learned,
The changes and things I've earned,
The aches and pains and stiffening kneed,
The people I've met and the places I've seen,
The joys that children and grandchildren bring;
More hope and happiness than anything.

Ears that are goofy,
Eyes that are loony,
Teeth that are not real
Make it hard to eat a decent meal.
These are what ate natural things:
Bodies that age and bones that creak.

But memories are the special things
And our faith that spirituality brings;
What we do with our mind
And treat others in kind,
Be good people throughout our days
And know that being good does pay.

Elva Sorensen

The Sandbox

Kid number 1 and kid number 2
Were playing in the sandbox,
And the grownups too.
Then they all fell asleep
Not aware that…..
Their toys would bounce and leap.
"Come with us" the toys said.
Let's go find treasure,
Where pirates tread.
Kid number 2 and kid number 1
Then woke up,
And the journey begun.
Wait! But what about kid number 3!
She may be small,
But she's just a baby.
Then they saw an X on the ground,
Next they started to dig,
Inside was a chest that was round.

AFTERWARD
They found treasure in bags and shared it all,
(will except with the toys).
I was kid 1 and this is my haul

Raegan Brimley

My High School

Wake up long before the sun,
Hit the floor on the run,
Just another long school day,
Where's my homework anyway.
I've got to get to my class,
Now my car is out of gas.
I need to borrow just a buck,
My sister tells me lots of luck.

One more day at my High
School,
Trying t earn the golden rule,
People screaming in my ear,
Telling me I just won't hear
Trying to give me their advice,
Never really thinking twice.
How much of this can I take,
I need a large mental break.

Bells ringing down the hall,
Bullies up against the wall.
Don't look them in the eye,
This is not my time to die.
Girls laughing at my hair,
Teachers stop just to glare.
Live my life for three o'clock,
Slam my books on the dot.

Jump in my car feel like a jerk,
Start her up and go to work.
Flipping burgers for the man,
Thinking about the future plan.
Paying taxes paying bills,
Making contacts making deals.
It all spins in my head,

As I pull myself to bed.

We turn around and start again,
Up and down there is no end.
This world we know is just a
place,
That spins around in outer space.
Then tomorrow is another day,
Doing things the same old way.
Life it takes us much too fast,
Soon everything we know is
past.

Joseph C. Sorensen

The City on the Hill

I.
A fortress stood
There on the hill.
Built in
Coarser times.

Built by men
With need to fear
Their enemies and climes.

Built of timber
Strong and thick.
Anchored deep
Joined and strong.

Built by men
And women who
Often sheltered
Often long.

Over years and
Over time
It grew in
Size and form.

Built to protect
And deflect
Both enemy
And storm.

In course of time
It served well;
Making strong
And secure.

Enemies were
Scattered, gone.
No longer
At the door.

II..
A city grew
On the hill
Anchored deep
On past years.

Soon forgotten
Was the strength
Hardened by
Trials and tears.

In comfort they
Lived their lives
Prosperous
And secure.

Happiness and
Safety givn'
By stalwarts
Gone before.

The sun itself
Grew warmer,
Even storms
Ceased to blow.

Forgotten was
The fierce time
Their fathers
Came to know.

The city grew;
Wealth and fame
Twas' known both
Far and wide.

Increased wealth brought
Ease of life
But also
Brought great pride.

Boasting, "Look what,
We have done,
Our city,
Oh so grand.

There is no one
To compare,
No one in
Any land."

Giving no thought
To future,
No notice
Of the past,

Only thoughts of
Pleasure now,
None thought it
Could not last.

"We sing, we feast,
All is well.
We lack for
Ner' a thing.

Lord and Lady,
Merchant, Priest,
All thought that
They were kings.

III…
There are creeping
Things in the
World that men
Disregard.

Unseen to those
With no sight
To those who
Keep no guard

Working slowly
Deep inside,
Cankerous
Creeping things;

Eat the heart from
Strong straight beams
And eat the
Hearts of kings.

Anchored timber
Once so strong
Weakened by
Marching time.

Crumbling to
Wormy dust,
Splintered, cracked,
Rot and grime.

IV….
Confident in
Their great worth,
Unaware,
Unafraid;

Long past the thought
That they should

Pay the price
Their fathers paid.

To take and use,
No intent
To rebuild
Or repay:

The city slept
Careless sleep
No thought of
Coming day.

The first great sound
From below
Gave no rise
To alarm.

No one thought the
City-Great
Could come to
Any harm.

Suddenly it
All gave way!
Collapsing
Deep within:

A roaring crash!
Plume of dust!
Tangled mass!
Awful din!

V…..
The march of time
Continues.
People travel
Too and fro'.

Few stop to ever
Wonder what
Happened here
Long ago.

Other cities
Have been raised;
Life goes on
As before.

On the hill a
Pile of dust,
Broken stone,
Nothing more.

A wind-blown mound
On the hill;
A warning
Mute and cold.

A message long
Forgotten
As the new
Replaces old.

John Sorensen

Three Little Pigs, Again

Huff and Puff and Chinee-chin-chin;
You're not in the country now.
The big Bad Wolf in a city of pigs
Dripped saliva from his jowls.

The first little pig, in ramshackle place
That just wasn't up to code.
At five stories tall and as fat as a pig
It leaned sidewise under the load.

The wolf huffed and puffed
And blew it back straight
Then it toppled on down
Bringing ham to his plate

The wolf tied up the pig
And headed downtown
To a brownstone apartment
That made the wolf frown

Great bricks had beaten him once
No matter how hard he had puffed
The second pig lived in a fortress of stone
Where his belly with feasts he stuffed

Now a wolf's senses are better than yours
And better than mine by far
And our wolf took hope and joy
When he saw the second pig's car

So instead of blowing the house
Until he ran right our of air
The wolf blew a terrible wind
Along the four tires and spare

The car lighted aloft and sailed upon high
And crashed deep into the wall
Right into the second pig's dining room
And the wolf got him, feast and all

Now the wolf should have been happy
With sausages and ham
But his tummy told him:
BACON
Into your mouth to cram

Now, the third little pig lived in a glass house
Designed to hold out the wind
So no matter how hard the wolf blew
Its walls he could not rend

18

So he climbed to the chimney
As he had once before
So the pig lit a fire
And made its flames to roar

But the wolf had a big rock
And he shattered the glass
Jumped through the hole
And then came to pass

The wolf praised the stone and
air
As he proudly lifted his fork
I truly am proud of my work this
day
And enjoy a trifecta of pork

Joshua P. Sorensen

Things I Love

I love my Mom and my Dad
I love that everywhere I go
They're always with me
I love playing
I love my stuffed animals
I love my blankies
I love my scriptures
I love my family
I love my house
I love drawing pictures and art
lessons
And I love playing my
Nintendo
I love playing soccer
I love painting
I love food and chocolate milk

Sawyer Brimley

Chapter 3 – 2016: Find your Family Tree

Child's Play

The children love to run and
play.
Their laughter fills the air.
Outdoor games throughout the
day.
The children love to run and
play.
Their faces shine in bright sun's
ray.
Tis joy beyond compare.
The children love to run and
play.
Their laughter fills the air.

Joshua P. Sorensen

Distance

Distance is the soft light
of unforeseen events
The melancholy melody
of painful past regrets

Distance is the ghost in front
Behind, its shadow stays
reminding of assumptions
now resting in its shade.

Putting Itself between,
two loved ones feel its sting.
But distance is a fond heart!
While not at once,
nor without tears
Reunion, it graciously imparts.

Amanda Bland

Fighting Ghosts

You came in the night
It was very dark
I could not see your face
But I felt an incongruence

With uneasy hands
I stabbed the dark
And then more urgently
But I was fighting ghosts

Phantoms swirling all around
Both night and day
The angst within the pain
without
How can you fight with ghosts?

Faces crowd the busy day
Loved and cherished all
I must protect them come what
may
And still I fight with ghosts

Children fear what lies ahead
When lessons should be learned
I will protect them come what
may
And still I fight with ghosts

My heart grows heavy my body
ill
Burdened with others; lessons
Deflected with dishonesty
And still I fight with ghosts

Years go by and children leave
They do not pack their lessons
Burdens aged are heavier yet
And still I fight with ghosts

Now I must face the truth within
No rescuer deflects my pain
Habits formed are heavy too
And still I fight with ghosts

To my dismay and strange relief
The ghost unveils its face
Will you bear my lessons too?
And still I fight with ghosts

I will protect you come what
may
This is the work I do
Come lay your lessons on my
back
And still I fight with ghosts

Now I have flung the burdens off
At last my body's free
From this day forth I stand for
me
And still I fight with ghosts

Susan Sorensen

☐

22

Grandma

Let me tell you about our
grandma,
She's in many ways like most,
She's generous and patient,
We're the only thing she boasts.

She enjoys the lot of us
Gathered all around,
And unless we're playing Pit
She's not bothered by the sound.

She loves to snuggle children
And read the story books
She always has a lot of treats
And plenty of bear hugs.

Most often she's just quiet,
Watching from her chair,
Or sitting on the front porch
Soaking up the summer air.

But every now and then
Her sense of humor on us
sneaks,
She cracks jokes we don't
expect
And at cards we think she
cheats.

Her wit is so surprising.
 It makes us laugh for sure
And like her quiet patience,
It's what makes her, her.

So she sits there and be's our
grandma,
Like someone said one day,
And we wouldn't have our
grandma
Any other way.

Jessica Brimley

23

My Heritage

"Oh little playmate,
Come out and play with me.
And bring your dollies three,
Climb up my apple tree.
Look down my rain barrel.
Slide down my cellar door.
And we'll be jolly friends,
Forever more!
Oh little playmate,
I can't come play with you.
My dolly has the flu.
Boo Hoo Hoo Hoo Hoo Hoo.
Ain't got no rain barrel,
Ain't got no cellar door,
But we'll be jolly Friends,
Forever More!"

Lap, clap, cross, clap, cross,
clap, both, clap,
Lap, clap, cross, clap, cross,
clap, both, clap.
And so it went, singing songs
with many names.
Playing faster and faster hand
clapping games.

Whiling away stretches of long,
hot drives;
Keeping my hands busy to not
scratch my hives.
We played and we sang when
bored out fishing,
Or keeping our minds off bellies
left hungry and wishing.

She'll be coming 'round the
mountain, and Down in the
Valley,
With many renditions of Country
Roads, and Red River Valley.
Songs and poems of loss and
hope
Were reminders that we were not
alone.

I think of the hours spent playing
Cat's Cradle
Waiting for dinner of pancakes
or soup from a ladle.
Playing board games and card
games round the table in a bunch
Eating mom's fresh pulled taffy,
pink popcorn, or crazy crunch.

I was too little to know we were
poor,
Compared to my friends, we had
so much more.
Dickens or Tolstoy, Sunday
afternoons were spent
Talking about Physics,
Astronomy, the news and events.

I've never regretted my
childhood for a minute,
Even though there were plenty
of "triggering events" within it.
I wasn't raised to be a victim or
resent pain and strife.
I was raised to be the hero of my
own life.

Morgan Templar

24

Love Bug

Paree is the place to be
When you're happy and in love.
But sometimes love is cruel.
You drool and you oversleep
too,
And eat too much ice cream
In boring America.
So listen to my saying or you'll
duel.
So go to Paree and be Happy
and in Love.

Anna Bland

Minecraft

You can turn a wolf into a dog,
and chop up a log.
You can turn ocelots into cats
and there's also cave bats.
There's ghast,
and the dragons are fast.
Baby zombies creep around at
night
and if you're in survival you
might get in a fight!
Villagers are annoying
with their "mmmms" and"
hmmmms".
There's very scary spiders
that you could count as
outsiders.

Sawyer Brimley

Mom's Poem

I have to write a poem, you see,
And hope that it makes sense,
A poet is not what I want to be,
But I will do my best.

First I need to find a topic
And make sure it rhymes,
With all the things swirling
Around in my mind.

Should it be sad or glad,
Or old or new?
Should it be fiction or fact,
Or barking or mewing?

Maybe it should be rainy or
shiny
Or hail, snow, or windy.
Or maybe about sports
Or horseracing.

Maybe it should be Clinton or
Trump
Or whoever decides to run.
One we can support or dump'
Or write someone in for fun.

How about all our kin?
Or neighbors and friends it could
be,
Or righteousness or sin,
To be tied down or be free.

Or maybe the Olympics in Rio
And the doping and drugs.
Is it healthy or sicko?
Or policemen or thugs?

Maybe it's vacation or school,
It could be insanity or fools.
Maybe it's flying cars or
Sign up for trips to Mars.

Or maybe it could be Zika
Or other kinds of bugs.
Bees, wasps, and flies,
Or maybe blue-jays or magpies.

Is it about more sugar or less?
Maybe more neatness or mess.
Maybe dark or more light,
Maybe more peace or fight.

I guess my mind is going crazy
In a body that wants to be lazy.

So my plan is to be happy
And enjoy all of my kids
(And grandkids and great-
grandkids, and great-great-
grandkids)
And do all of my puzzles and
books,
And, of course, my cat.

Elva Sorensen

26

Moonlight Walk

A walk in the moonlight
Past a fish pond
He'll take you at midnight
To make a special bond

Through the gate
And out to the trees
You can hear
All the birds, crickets, and
bees

Into a clearing
The moon shines down bright
The moment is nearing
On this beautiful night

A bench and a swing
Your heart fills with glee
Then he pulls out a ring
"Will you marry me?"

Karleigh Brimley

Nature's Homily

In Memoria: Josiah Sorensen
(written on 8 Jun 2016 his first
Birthday after his passing)

Ascend the desert highlands,
Through canyons and the hills
And live amongst the scrub oaks,
Juniper and sage.

Travel by the waters,
The winding mountain rills.
Spending time in nature
Tis a golden age.

The animals are graceful
Drinking from the river bends.
Your fire, it is warm
And keeps out night-time chill.

Spending time with family.
Laughing with your friends.
A homily of enjoyment
And eternal weal!

Joshua P. Sorensen

Shortbread Kisses

Rush and run go and move.
I must go to, then to fro.
Time is short, the sun low.
Boxes check and lists cross,
Busy be or all is lost.

Little ears.
Little eyes.

Yes, Yes, you are important.
Not just now too much to do.
Sorry, love, it's all for you.
No stopping, no pause;
Must outpace the waiting jaws…

Little face.
Little teeth.

When things are calm!
Stuff needs stuffing,
Things need thinging.
Hurry and wait,
not yet: too late!

Little nose.
Little voice.

Of course, my dear,
Please just wait,
I cannot bate,
I cannot slow,
I cannot slow.

Little cheeks.
Little kiss.

Shortbread breath,
cookie sweet.
Little hands.

You pause me,
and I rest a while.

Aaron Davis

☐

Roses Are Red

Roses are red
Irises are blue
You love me
And I love you too

Lucus Millet

The Poetry Contest

One day as I was thinking of
what to do,
I thought I'd write a poem for
you.
And as I pondered what to say,
I said "should it be about a girl
named May?"

"No!" I exclaimed that would
be too silly,
"What about a boy named
Willy?"
"Yes!" I shouted with all my
glee,
"And what if that little girl was
me?"

"Now what next?"
I said perplexed.
"Well I'll go get the mail and
when I come back,"
"I'll look through the entire
stack."
On top was a little letter,
"This one should make me feel a
little better."

************************+

++++
COME TO A POETRY
CONTEST
AT 300 EAST 900 WEST
MAYBE YOUR POEM WILL
BE THE BEST

IT'S AT 10 AFTER 2
THE SKY WILL BE BLUE
CALL US AT (8##)###-8222

1:00 So as I finished up my
rhyming
The church bell started chiming.
"It's 1:00." He said to me,
You better get going so you see.
To get to the park took an entire
hour,
But I also smelt good because I
took a shower.

Later, when reading my poem to
the others,
I heard lots of "Oh brothers."

As I kept reading, I thought in
my head
"They must think their poems
are dead,"
I won that contest some years
ago,
And now I have something to
show.

Raegan Brimley

The Heroes' Path

The road is long.
The day is long.
The night is long.
The hero has struggled into a
rocky path and lost his way,
Fog, brambles, and thorns rise
up to thwart his every step.

Has the world forsaken?
Has the earth forsaken?
Has the Guide forsaken?
"No" a quiet Voice calls out to
me "Be patient and yet stay,"
"I will comfort and guide him
home. Long for his safety you
have wept."

I heard the Voice
I knew the Voice.
I believed the Voice.
The Guide and Comforter
cannot lie. And the Hero had
soon come home.
"Oh what joy!" we the hero's
loved ones, shouted from our
very hearts.

Shout Hosanna!
Sing to Hosanna!
Praise to Hosanna!
But wait. Our singing was cut
short and the path was not yet
won.
In the very hallelujah the Debtor,
that final debtor, came to seize
his part.

[Groan!]

The hero has fallen.
The brother has fallen.
The beloved has fallen.
I dropped to the earth and wept;
for in the midst of joy the hero
ends his fight.
Now, I cannot, no I will not, ever
again open my weeping eyes.

The stars should weep.
The moon should weep.
The sun should weep,
And they also, in sorrow should
forever shield their light.
How could they, how would
they, choose to do otherwise?

Another day will pass.
Another night will pass,
Time herself will pass.
Yet, still I will lay in the dust
and I will refuse to look on to
their garish show.
Oh, where is the Guide? He
promised our hero our brother,
would now be free.

[Weep]

"Arise from the dust,"
Arise From the Dust!"
ARISE FROM THE DUST!!"
Thrice the Voice calls to me
from sorrow's lonely shore.
The Voice, who outshines all the

30

light, in a silent and thunderous
voice speaks:

"I had lost my Lamb."
"I did seek my lamb."
"I have found my lamb."
"And I will hold him in my
eternal arms forever more,
The Guide does not forsake, but
with perfect love will always
seek."

[Rejoice!]

Shout Hosanna!
Sing to Hosanna!
Praise to Hosanna!
From the dust I will rise, for I
too am sought by the Guide.
My footsteps will seek out all the
heroes who before have gone.

Let the stars shine.
Let the moon shine.
Let the sun shine.
For with a far greater light then
they, my soul will now abide.
I will follow the heroes' path
and, with the Guide, they will
lead me home.

Rhea Cragun

**Note from thePoem's
author**: Over the last month or
so my mind has been given to
much reflection on family and
the plan of salvation. I have been
thinking of those we have lost in
this life: Josiah, Jill, Dad, little
Isaac, our Samantha, and
Robert's twin brother Ron, who
we lost so long ago. And all the
others who have gone on before
us.
*As I was contemplating this I
remembered what the officiator
said when we had our Samantha
sealed to us. He stated that she
needed this ordinance so that
she could go on and grow and
do the things she needed to do. I
know of a surety that one of
those things was to prepare to
meet Josiah and Jill and be a
guide to them through their next
steps in the eternal plan.
From this contemplation came
this poem.*
-   Rhea Cragun

31

Chapter 4 – 2017: Harry Potter

Curse of The Black Clock

An old, abandoned cottage on a
hill painted white,
Where five lost children sought
refuge in the night…

Four saw a home, but the fifth
saw a cell.
And every single morning he
would wake up to a bell:
"One o'clock! One o'clock," the
black clock tocked –
Its paint chipped away
where the others saw a polish –
Only chiming once a day,,,

And his ears would ring 'til the
noise was but a dream,
Falling back into a deeper
sleep…

An old, abandoned garden by the
cottage painted brown,
Where the first lost child got
sucked into the ground…

She had seen a home, but the
fifth had seen a cell.
And every single morning he
would wake up to a bell:
One o'clock! One o'clock," the
black clock tocked –

"I'll take you all away until
there's no one left!
Just see how long you'll stay…"

And his ears would ring 'til the
noise was but a dream,
Falling back into a deeper
sleep…

An old, abandoned river passed
the garden painted green,
Where the next lost child got
swept out of the scene..

She had seen a home, but the
fifth had seen a cell,
And every single morning he
would wake up to a bell:
"One o'clock! One o'clock," the
black clock tocked –
A blessing was the way to
escape these halls.

Skye Caden

Dragons

A dragon flies high in the sky,
Joining with friends the battle is
nigh.
The men are raging trying to kill,
The dragons are sure that blood
will be spilt.
The men will make armor and
weapons too,
While the dragons all wait for
the cue.
The men are nearing, the
dragons take flight,
The time has come for them to
fight.
But one dragon steps out of the
fight,
Trying to make friends, hoping
he might.
The friendly dragon got bumped
and pushed
Up and down the field,
Until a human came
And protected him with his
shield.
The dragon has now made a
friend,
Soon the battle will end.
They both went back to blow
their horns.
The dragons retreat and become
airborne.
While the humans all ran back to
their castle.
And they all celebrate the end of
this hassle.

Sawyer Brimley

Monster's Feast

While Trolls dream of supper
The Ogres, flesh do rip.
Werewolves love human hearts,
And Vampires take a sip.

But there is one creature,
As Zombies oft complain,
That eats every morsel
In their gluttonous reign.

It is the gruesome Maggot,
The youthful Lord of Flies.
Will munch on your innards
And squirm out from your eyes.

Oft preferring dead flesh
Yet will eat live meat too.
And when you pass away,
They will come for you.

Joshua P. Sorensen

34

Dream

I dashed through the courtyard
running away,
There was a dragon behind me
for I was its prey.
Then a wizard appeared and
lightning shot from his staff,
I think he came here on my
behalf.
Thus I turned around and there I
saw,
What was left of the dragon was
one little claw.
"Keep it." Said the wizard,
"For there will soon be a
blizzard."
"There are monsters so
dangerous, ferocious, and mean.
"You must have a weapon and
you have to be keen."
So I made a spear out of the
claw,
And then in the bushes I spotted
a paw.
A werewolf jumped out,
So I started to shout.
The wizard had vanished,
And I was famished.
So I turned around and started to
run.
But soon it became two on one.
A vampire in front a werewolf
behind,
A tall stone wall was all I could
find.
So I climbed to the summit,
Then I started to plummet.

I fell down, down, down past a
meadow lark,
Then suddenly everything went
dark.
Amazed at all the things I had
seen,
I realized it was all just a dream.

Unknown

Tree

I am life.
Light moves through me,
letting my heart beat.
I feel the sun on my skin,
my hair, sending power to
my veins.
I feel life between my toes.
Every creature that walks by
I sense.
I never see, always feel,
bringing life to me, and to
life I give back.

Shannon Millet

35

Family Poetry

With story or emotion,
With tall tale or song,
Poets speak of life and living,
In this world where we belong.

Jack London with his tales,
Of the treacherous frozen north,
Tennyson whose heroes,
Help us see what life is worth.

Dickenson and Wordsworth,
Sharing beauty that they see,
In nature, in humankind,
Sets our spirits free.

Some use verse to free or soothe,
An aching soul or broken heart,
To give release from slaving pain,
To find a way to a new start

Whether joy or pain or fear,
To poke some fun or question why,
To make a point or praise the Lord,
To give a laugh or breathe a sigh;

Paper marked by thoughtful pen,
The heartfelt verse, the crafted
word;
No better way to speak the heart,
No better way that thoughts are
heard.

So when we gather here today,
To share our thoughts with those we
love,
We share a stage with greatness,
We share an ancient trove.

Everyone who speaks today,
Everyone who reads a poem,
Is adding to our family's name,
To our story, to our tome.

My sister, my grandchild,
My nephew, my niece,
All sharing words from the heart,
Give me comfort, give me peace.

Wisdom from my mother,
Humor from my son,
My daughter reminiscing,
I love them everyone.

I put you on a pedestal,
Above Browning or Wordsworth,
Above Tennyson or Frost.
To me you all have greater worth.

Honest thoughts from a child,
Are more precious to me,
Than all the famous poets,
In all their reverie.

Let us remember what's important,
As we live our lives each day,
It's the living poem of family,
What we do and what we say.

John Sorensen

Spring

It's a wonderful thing,
This thing we call spring.
Some places it rains and snows,
And hails and blows,
All in one day,
You know.
You can ski and swim and play
A round of golf,
All on the same day.
Hiking and climbing and just go
play.

The flowers come and go,
Because of the cold snow.
Lilacs frozen on the spot,
Next day it's hot.
Don't plant until Mother's Day,
The frost is supposed to be gone
so;
All those things that are in the
pot;
In the ground they go,
Hoping the sun will be hot.
Mow the lawn, weed the garden
plot,
Clean the fish pond….No, wait,
it's not hot!
Snow on the ground,
It's like a merry-go-round.
Apricots and cherries did freeze,
Hay fever time; runny nose and
sneeze.
Oh no! Middle of May and it
snowed all day.
Ah well, what can I say?

Summer – people on the move,
Like migrating birds.
Rhea and Robert to Iowa went,
David and Lindsey from
Washington came,
Lynn out of Rock Springs came,
Josh and Brian found an
apartment to rent.

Finally we can plant and sigh,
Frost is gone, flowers can
bloom,
Oh no!
We have snow!
Alas, doom and gloom,
Halfway into June.

Planted more pots,
Did more weeding, that's a lot.
Weather is getting hot.
Sprinklers are shot.
Can't cut the lawn while,
The sprinklers are getting fixed.
Cleaning the garage is thrown in
the mix.

Finally the day comes
That we can get on the ball.
Planted more flowers, ready for
fall.
Sprinklers are running.
Now, broken pipes!
Replace valves!
Adjust heads to overlapping,
Keep an eye on so no napping.

Snakes

Summer is here, Hurray!
Hot hot days and wind.
Ah, feels so good today.
That's why we love living here.
Our lakes and mountains so dear.
Fishing and hiking,
Let's make that clear.
No snow or frost,
A day to play at any cost.

Reunion time is here.
Families get together to win the points
That's on the agenda of games and sports.
Visiting and eating and playing,
Cousins, Aunts, Uncles and friends,
And anyone else who wants to come.
Enjoying life and each other,
And thank God,
For all these blessings.

Elva Sorensen

There are snakes inside my belly
It is not warm from radiation
Poisonous snakes inside my body
They create the heat
The snakes warm my body
Poisonous snakes radiate heat

They are like giant worms
Dangerous venom
Dangerous snakes
Got rid of them a long time ago
Years ago

Giant worm-thing
Very big
Super log
It is a big snake
Still inside my body
Creates this heat
Like radiation sickness
It burns

These big giant worms, radiating
Stuck inside my body
This is a nightmare
This kills me
It is dangerous

Brian Mealing

Poetry

I think I'll rely on what comes from
this pen –
And hope that my words don't bore
or offend.

After all how hard can it be
To write a great poem just look
around and see.

This group of fine people, this
Sorensen family tree –
Is made up of those who might
possibly be

The finest and best
The cream of the crop
So let's get on with the contest till
we decide who's on top.

Okay I put it off
I have only got three days
I have to find great words
But my mind's in a haze –

Where's the lyric
The prose, The haiku
Where's the genius if only I knew.

How to write a poem
It's just a few words
I've got at least three hours
Until Don gets home.

He won't write one
Though it's his schtick
He thinks he'll
Get away with
A cheesy limerick.

But not in this group
Not with you folk
You have some talent
You're all too well-spoke

There's John with his humor
Mom with her wit
Josh and Sky who do the poetry
club bit.

Why even the kids have excellent
rhymes
I've heard them recite
Some amazing lines

So how am I to earn the prize
If I can't come up with something
clever and wise.

I know, I'll get the thesaurus
I'll get out the books
I'll write some big words I'll find
clever hooks-

Or maybe I'll try some sad somber
tale
That exposes a side that you don't
know so well –

No there's risk in that,
you might judge my soul
Or sit there a thinking my poem is
quite dull.

But humor is not as easy I think
As John makes it look.
I'm sure mine would stink.

Mary Mealing

39

Voices

I am made of voices.

Some with sticks,
Some with stones,
Some hit home
With loving tones.

Words now blurred
From end to start,
the voices ring
in choral parts.

The bully, the friend,
teachers, T.V.
Each have added
their voices to me.

Mas and Pas
Both norm and grand
Have given form
To heart and mind.

Reflecting back
With smile or shudder
On marks I've left
With idle utter.

Now I pray
To ever be
A voice soft, kind
And lovely.

We are the sum of voices.

Aaron Davis

Refuge

I'll build a towering mountain peak,
And on its shadowed shoulders cast
A thousand hidden fountain seeps

Among a silhouette of trees
That sail the sky like unfelled masts
Upon the towering mountain peak

I'll also carve a desert keep
Where remnant stone records the past
And hides a thousand fountain seeps

Tor those who from the canyon seek
A refuge in the furnace blast:
A metaphoric mountain peak,

Within whose towering depths repeat
The memory of shadows cast
by prehistoric fountain seeps,

Where heart and soul together meet
And find a future in the past:
Upon the towering mountain peak
Or hidden where the fountains seep.

Lynn Sorensen

10 Alliteration Iterations

Of world leaders, telltale tale is
told Presidents, current ones, not
ones once of old

Present Presidents
who went to gather, together to
behold

Preset present Presidents
and benevolent the two, too, to
bestow

Present present Presidents
present
well, well, welfare fair on the
poor

Present present Presidents
present peasants
not moments past, no, now,
know

Present present Presidents
presently present peasants
presents
each one won one gift gifted

Present present Presidents
presently present pleasant
peasants present presents
that before had had been
shipped,

Present present Presidents
presently preset peasants present
presents
to the quick, quickly quicken
sovereigned scowl

Present present Presidents
presently preset pleasant
peasants present presents
each with withered, red, wild-
game fowl.

Present present Presidents
presently present
pleasant peasants present
pheasant presents

Jason J Sorensen

Picture

A blank paper
A pen
Some color
And then

One   [?blurred]
One   [?blurred]
Clock ticks
Don't stop

A picture emerges
A beautiful sight
The gold medal is won
You did it, all right!

Karleigh Brimley

41

Pigs

They come every night, those big
wild pigs.
I have no defenses, but my blanket
in my crib.
I hear them grunt and snarl and
cry,
As they slink under the beds of
my sisters who are nigh.
I'm worried that my sisters might
be eaten up.
I pray and hope no sister wakes or
gets up.
No crying out loud or even to fret.
If the pigs hear me, I might get
'et.
Sometimes there is one,
sometimes there are four,
Sometimes there could be even a
few more.
There's nothing I can do but cry,
whimper and sob,
I can't even call Hyope, our good
old dog.
Sometime in the morning, as the
light starts to rise,
Those hogs disappear, right before
my eyes.
I wake up to daylight, the danger
has past
Until the next night. I hope this
won't last.
Now as a memory I understand
more,
There were no hogs, just sisters
who snore.

Morgan Templar

Why Old Bill Camped alone

Old Bill loved to camp more
than anything else.
He loved the mountains, deserts,
rivers and lakes.
Outdoors was better than indoors
for heaven sakes.

Any chance he could, Bill snuck
out with his gear;
Hiking and fishing in wilderness
without fear.

Bill camped alone more often
than not,
but no one knew why or gave it
much thought.

Once in a while a friend would
ask Bill, "can I go along too?"
But Bill wouldn't commit to
him, or follow through,

Finally, his friend would give
up, and then off Bill would go;
happy to explore new places
wandering around solo.

As the years went by, Bill's
friends began wondering why
they were never invited.
They puzzled over the great
camping stories Bill told and a
mystery was incited.

Why does Bill go camping
alone? Without his friends and
family?
The stories he told inspired
them; made them laugh, even
filled them with envy.

Finally, a small group of Bill's
friends got together and
determined,
We just have to get Bill to take
us camping.

But what is the best way to get
him to commit?
Do we plead with him, trick him,
or just throw a fit?

"why don't we follow him out
there one day?
One said. "We can surprise him
and then he will be force to
welcome our stay!"

So that became their plan, and
that's when they conspired to be
ready the next time they saw Bill
packing to go.
they too would not be far behind
him, tracking his movements
both high and low.

Up and down mountains, across
deserts they would scatter;
To follow their friend to the ends
of the earth was no matter.

They didn't have to wait long
you see, just a few days later Bill
got that familiar look in his eye;
It was time once again to camp
under an open sky.

His friends caught Bill's look
and made their own
preparations.
They were quiet and stealthy and
ready to launch their surprise.
They'd follow him out there,
then Bill would have no choice
but to laugh was his friends'
great surmise.

Early the next morning Bill
pulled out of his driveway, not
noticing the car following far
behind him.
He drove into the mountains
with a pile of camp stuff happy
and without care.
Up into the mountains the two
vehicles drove, his friends
careful not to let Bill know they
were there.

At last, Bill drove into a clearing
and stopped his truck
Was this the best moment to
announce their pluck?

No, they affirmed, we should
watch for awhile first,
Then we could invade Bill and
his campsite with our outburst.

So they waited and watched, as
Bill unloaded his gear.
Out came his tent, sleeping bag
and non-alcoholic beer.

But then he pulled something
strange from his truck bed,
A case of beans and then another
and anther until they were
stacked as tall as his head.

"What in the world!" exclaimed
the concealed little group.
"That's enough beans to make
an army poop!

What is Bill doing out here with
all those beans…surely he can't
possibly plan too eat 'em all?"
Why there's enough cans to last
him clear to next Fall!

The little group puzzled and
pondered this scene until they
could no longer take it.
All at once they rushed into
Bill's camp yelling "Surprise!"
Bill startled, jumped up from his
seat and gasped quite a bit.

"What are YOU guys doing
here?!" Bill said,
With a hint of disappointment
and dread.

We wanted to surprise you and
join your adventure!
We followed you here cuz we
never got an invite –

Sorry if we gave you a big
fright.

Well, Bill exclaimed, now that
you're here, I guess it's okay.
We can go fishing, hiking, and I
have some cards we can play.

So the friends settled in for a few
days of fun.
Soon it was lunch time and they
were all hungry,
Joe and Bob brought out ham
sandwiches and Ted ate peanut
butter and honey.

They watched as Bill opened a
can of his bean and put them in a
pot.
Joe had to ask, "Bill , what's
with all the beans?"
And Bill shyly said, "I just like
them a lot!"

He heated them up on his
Coleman camp stove,
And soon the smell of baked
bans wafted above this cove.

The others were content to sit
there and munch
Pondering the stack of beans
during their lunch.

As the days went by, the friends
camped with Bill noted his
curious diet;
No matter what mealtime it was

he ate beans, until none of them could stay quiet.

One night around the campfire, Bob finally asked,
"Bill, why do you eat beans for breakfast, lunch, and dinner?"
Then they all laughed.

"I don't know why really, I just like their taste."
But secretly Bill hated the critique that he faced.

He knew it was odd to crave beans when he camped, which was one reason why he never invited these guys.
It was easier to go camping alone than face questions of this wise.

Bill wanted to keep his beans secret. He really liked beans – so what if it was strange to his friends.
He didn't concern himself with what message it sends,

This all had an effect on poor Bill and his stomach started to rumble.
It built slowly at first, but Bill's tummy noises grew loader.
His friends looked at each other "What was that?!"
When a great gurgle was heard around the fire.

Bob laughed and pointed at Bill "he's going to blow!
Too many beans will kill you" he said, but little did he know.

Bill was embarrassed his face turning red, but it wasn't this emotion that consumed his head
His stomach was boiling and not happy at that moment
His bean diet was really starting to foment.

The campfire friends talked and joked, not noticing Bill's growing distress.
If Bill didn't get out of there fast, he was going to make a huge mess!

And then…as Bill started to rise,
His unsuspecting friends , and nearby forest creatures got an immense surprise!

FARRRRRRRRRRRRT!
It was by any measure, the loudest fart ever heard.

Bill was stunned by its thunder.
When he turned to look at his friends, he was awestruck by wonder.

Not one of them was there.
It was as if they had all vanished into thin air!

For hours Bill wandered around
looking in the dark'
He searched for them with shout
after shout.
But it wasn't until next morning
he realized –

The campfire and his friends had
been blown out!

Be Aware of Beans!

Don Mealing

Chapter 5 – 2018: Going to Space

The Talk

The talk is something we all
need to know.
The things to help us as we
grow:

When being introduced to the
elderly, you need to stand,
Remove your hat when shaking
their hand.

And:

Remove your hat when
entering someone's home;
Wipe the feet before crossing
the doorway.
Always say "excuse me" when
walking in front of someone;
"Please" and "thank you" are
always nice to say.

Always wash hands and face,
and comb your hair
Before sitting down to eat at
the table.
If you are on a date, hold the
chair for her to sit;

And girls, always let them be
courteous, especially when
they are able.

When you are driving the car,
Be nice to the others who are
driving too:
Even if you are in a hurry, they
are too.

Be patient and kind and smile a
lot.
Don't be sarcastic and rude,
And no "I'm just joking!"

"If you chance to see a frown,
Do not let it stay.
Quickly turn it upside down
And smile that frown away.

No one likes a frowny face.
Turn it to a smile.
Make the world a better place
By smiling all the while."

Now remember "The Talk"!

Elva Sorensen

Black Beans

In the land where I was born I
helped my grandma plant the
beans
They climbed upon the
cornstalks to touch the morning
light
When the soldiers came to steal
that land I was just a tender
child
They said "don't make us hunt
and shoot you, by putting up a
fight"

"Most likely you will be
walking so take only what you
can"
Within the pouch tied round
my waist I slipped a tiny bean
Shedding tears I took the hand
of my ill and aged grandma
We turned our faces towards a
land that we had never seen

As we crossed the Smokey
Mountains it began to snow
We were tired and harshly
driven along "The Trail Where
They Cried"
With corn to eat we struggled
on, suffering illness and
starvation
One bitterly cold and snowy
night I watched my grandma
die.

Caressing the bean in the pouch
at my waist brought me precious
memories of her
I vowed that I would survive this
march and when I reached my
new home
I would find a good place, plant
it with care, as she taught me
years ago.
I believed that this was my only
hope to restore me and make me
whole.

The land where they led us was
dismal and bleak with very little
water
I found a small plot where the
moisture was sparse and then
prepared the soil
I carefully planted my little bean
then prayed that it would
flourish
A few weeks later I saw a sprout,
a testament of my toil

I am old and for memory's sake,
I yearly plant one little black
bean
From my childhood bean,
countless thousands, are
harvested every year
That little black bean so
carefully planted has spread
across the land
A living monument to those who
walked the Cherokee Trail of
Tears

Susan Sorensen

48

Poem Pirates

I wish I was a pirate,
"Arr!" like Smee and Captain
Hook.
I want the bootie for myself
I would capture merchants
And make them walk the
plank.
I want to sing shanties.
"Yo ho, Yo ho, the pirate's like
for me."
I don't remember the middle
part, but:
"Yo ho, Yo ho, the pirate's life
for me."

But there is dangers a plenty,
my maties:
Pirate curses on the bootie,
The kraken and triton,
Swimming octopus will grab
me,
And the screaming water of
doom,
Thar she blows.
From a sea serpent's heart
To a giant crab's claws,
I'm scared of the sea,

Brian Mealing

Life in The Woods

You and me have so much to
see
It's like a tree observed by a
bumble-bee
but when I die I will cry and
say good-bye-
And happiness is to see.

Lucas Bland

49

The Grandma Game

All the family gathers 'round
It's that time of day,
when you can win toys and
prizes,
it's The Grandma Game!

The children bounce with
excitement
for the games in store.
While the grownups sit and
wait
for home supplies galore.

The pans are in the circle,
they're comin' 'round to you.
You hope you roll some
doubles,
to get that glitter glue.

"Or maybe I'll get a game,"
you say,
"That jungle Go Fish! Looks
fun."
Then something else catches
your eye,
a giant nerf spray gun.

Smiling you pick up the dice,
it's time to win a prize.
You toss the dice into the pan-
it's a four and a five. ☹

Karleigh Brimley

Rhinos In Motion

Anthropomorphic Rhinos Fight
Comic Ninja Leaps through the
Air
Hoping to Qin Maiden's Delight
Anthropomorphic Rhinos Fight
White Crane Rhinos are Quite a
Sight
It Makes the People Stop and
Stare
Anthropomorphic Rhinos Fight
Comic Ninja Leaps through the
Air

Joshua P Sorensen

☐

My Name Is

Yo, my name is Joe
I was sitting in the snow
I was eating a sloppy-joe
Yo, Pinocchio
Came and took my sloppy-joe
Then Mario came
And said yo-yo-yo-yo!

Liam Davis

Hymn

(sung to the melody 'Children of Our Heavenly Father")

All I have the Lord has given,
Life on earth and hope of
heaven.
All the things I love and treasure
He apportions without measure;

Shall I then, when I am bidden,
Hide the treasure He has given?
Selfishly withhold the offering
That was purchased by His
suffering?

Nay, I'll give my treasure freely,
It was never mine for keeping.
I will lay my heart before Him,
What he gave, I would restore
him.

Lynn Sorensen

My Favorite Part of School

I love to read and write,
But I'd rather not get into a
fight.

Math is fun, grammar too,
But I don't want to chew a
shoe,

Vocabulary comes with logic
puzzles,
But I don't want to lick their
muzzles.

I think about spelling and
Spanish,
But I don't think I'm famished.

Piano goes ding dong,
And that's my little song.

Sawyer Brimley

The Great Digest

With no time to tell, I would
much rather sum -
For hasty is better than tasty in
tum –
The story of all our good by rule
of thumb,
Rebellion to quell in one all
sense of yum.

It started with rumbling,
tumbling sound
When we had the urges to scarf
our lunch down,
But the first tiny bite was then
soon to astound,
For our meal had the notion of
running around!

Meat jumped off the table and
shattered the plates
And the veggies weren't willing
to negotiate.
The fruits were too slippery,
fingers too late,
And sugar had lost us at salivate.

Our bellies so empty, we all
soon collapsed,
And our escapee meal saw its
chance to attack!
Food nibbled and munched and
chomped and smacked,
And saw us as nothing but prime
baby back.

And that is the story of
mankind's doom,
For prey hunted predator in
every room.
Remember this story, my dear
distant friends,
Because once it begins, a bad
scoop never ends.

Skye Caden

I Wish I Could Change the Past

I wish I could change the past
And the coming future.
I feel like leaving,
Going to a space and time
When everyone is well.

I wish we could bring back the
dead,
Once the Apocalypse happens
And Jesus comes forever,
We could start over again,
Like when I was born.

Brian Mealing

The Poetry Contest

I was sitting on my bed, thinking
what to do,
When I thought that I would
write a poem for you.
But what should my poem be
about?
The topic is what I need to figure
out.
So.......
I could do something like Josh
and Skye,
Something about horror and
things that die.
Like Rhea I could write about
killing Rudolph,
Or I could write about melting
Olaf.
I could follow after Sawyer and
write about puppies,
Or I could write about dragons
or guppies.
What if I write about stinky
socks?
What if I write about
Goldilocks?
What bout Black Friday like me
Dad?
Oh, the fun that he had.
Or, like Karleigh, a cherry tree,
I can't think of anything. Don't
you see?
The contest came and I was sad,
Because this is all that I had.

Raegan Brimley

Time

Sitting on the sandy shore
A glass for hours set before.
The sand ponders down
And multitudes rest around.

No rush, no want,
A restful, playful, pace.
No notice of the coming race.

Then comes the waves,
Whisking time away,
Leaving naught but rock to stay.

Now with speed the hours pass
by,
Panic, fears, and want
No time! No time!
I rush to fill the empty fill,
The sand now rare
The lack of still.
No hour to spare.

Life is lost to rush and need
Peace gives way to reckless
speed.
No sand, no time,
Not even thyme.
A single crystal
In my hand
An empty glass
To pass – no more.

Aaron Davis

53

Goblins

One dark and stormy night
The sky was full of fright.
The wind was blowing hard,
And the clouds were torn and
scarred.
A rumble shook the ground,
All the dogs barked in the
pound.
With madness in their eyes
They howled their mournful
cries.
While the children hid in fear
The warden plugged her ear.
Across the muddy field
Where the dogs go to be killed,
Stood an old abandoned house
In which goblins would carouse.
The warden, in her fright,
Ran screaming through the
night.
Straight to the haunted hall
And crouched within the walls.
Sliding slowly up behind her,
(Let me give you a reminder):
The goblins, with their wicked
eyes.
Planned to take her by surprise.
The warden turned and saw them
there,
And woke up screaming in her
chair.

Lynn Sorensen

The Sly Troll

One fine day in the pumpkin
bed,
When the leaves were turning
brown,
A baby troll poked up his head
And slyly looked around.

The first thing that mean baby
spied
Was the farmer's pussy cat,
A calico, with yellow eyes,
Asleep upon a mat.

He sneaked behind that lazy
thing,
And softly, to her tail,
He tied a piece of colored string
And hooked it to a pail.

He gave the colored string a
yank
And off the kitty ran,
The bucket followed it with a
clank
Like an empty gallon can.

The farmer's cat ran round and
round
The Jack-o-lantern patch,
While the baby troll sat on the
ground
And laughed and laughed and
laughed.

Lynn Sorensen

Eastering

Early in the morning
When the sun is coming up,
All the birds start singing
And wake the children up.

They quickly jump out of their
beds
To find their Easter stuff,
They laugh and shake their silly
heads,
But can't look hard enough,

Because the Easter Bunny
Has hid them all so well.

(We know where to find them
But promised not to tell!)

Then all the kids and parents too
Are off to Grandma's place
To hunt for eggs around the
yard:
Just see their smiling face!

Then, if the weather's good and
bright
We all begin to beg.
To go out to the desert
And roll our Easter Eggs!

Lynn Sorensen

55

Chapter 6 – 2019: Viking Tales

Unusual Love Between the Clover and the Dove

Once upon a time, wait…This needs to rhyme. Let's start over, This story is about a clover. Once the clover had met a dove that flew above. Then the dove became a friend with the clover and then the clover lend the dove information. Then the dove had repaid. Then they made pictures as they laid in the shade. Then the clover and dove…were in love. Then they met Ben who was friends with an army of men. And then the dove went with the men with Ben. They needed to fight an army called The Sacred Bite. Then when they fought, and before that, the dove had bought a gift with a note saying, "If I die please Don't Dry." This was for the colover named Lily Then Lilly found out that the dove had died and yes, the clover named Lily did indeed cry. Then the clover was picked and got a new friend. The End.

Unknown

Majestic Cats

I am a cat. A gorgeous cat.
Look at me go. Wow so awesome sitting on keys.
My perfect jumpt, there's nothing wrong abou me, nothing at all. Sleeping in your plants, eating your meats and cakes. Aren't I pretty? Aren't I fast? Sleepin in faces, don't you love it?
  And when I do that Hiss, I'm so proud. And when I bring in birds and mice you're so glad. Stretching and napping in the sun. Chasing my tail, oh so fun. Mothing bad about me, nothing at all. Those leaps, prances, jumps and more. Cats of America galore!
  Wait, is that a ball of yarn?!

Unknown

Dragon Doom

LO! The sun sets, casting colors in the West.
In our days of peace the sun always shines.
In the night are no demons, few are our fears.
But many have memories of terrible times.
Of fear and lost fortune, of lost lands.
Of many lost men, of women wielding weapons.
Of panic laden paths for our children.

In those times there came a monster to men.
Bringing fear to families, crushing the country.
A huge dragon bringing death, death and destruction.
Death to all it found and fought, attacking any not hidden away.
A dragons attack may be slow and secret or open and overwhelming.
It burned our buildings and carried our cattle to its hidden hole.

It brought fear to our folks and death to our devoted friends.
In those days of disaster, many searched for strength and fame.
Lost was many a man who fought and found,

His strength and skill were not enough.
Many fought for family, many protected the people.
Here were heroes, giving life for love of kin and country.
In times of terror some lose their lives,

But some wind, their way walking in doubtful directions.
Searching for the hidden hoard; the dragon's devilish treasure.
Wanting more than man should they lose their lives in unwanted ways.
Many a man was lost searching for the huge hoard in the dragon's den.
Not caring or not knowing that when taking wicked treasure,
One becomes the beast that hid the hoard.

I was one that became trapped searching this treasure.
Loving my family and home but still wandering in the wild.
Building deceit but also defeat, desiring my own hoard.
I was a king with many kin.
My good queen kept my home and kept kinfolk secure.
I loved my manor, loved life with my queen,
But loathed to leave the dragon domain,

58

I was becoming the beast.
I felt my heart change, I was
digging deeper,
Into the treacherous trap of a
dragon's doom,
Losing heart, losing home,
losing my road to recovery.
But duty overcame desire, one
last chance I chose:
To right my recklessness, to save
my soul, to keep the kingdom,
I chose to fight the fiend, to
destroy the dragon.

I set out searching for the
dragon's den.
I searched mountain and
meadow, canyon and cave, forest
and fiord.
Until by fortune I found the
lethal beast's lair.
I watched it wing down to a
crevice in a canyon as mornings
sun first shown.
Here I made my camp as I
waited and wondered,
How to defeat the dragon and
save my soul.

As the sun set the evil one
emerged.
I rushed toward the tyrant before
it gushed and gained its first fire.
With broad blade I beat at its
body, thrust at its throat.
I fiercely fought.
But movement and muscle, hard
skin and scale,

Blocked my savage sharpened
steel.
Then claws came at me
shattering my shield, flailing me
forward to the ground.
Ripped from my hand my blade
bounced into the canyon's
crevice.
The lizard lunged forward,
inhaling, preparing to produce its
first flame.
In desperation I drew my
scraema sax.
I swung my sax splitting the
nose between nostrils, blood
burst out.
Flame started forth but blood
boiled in its throat.
Flame caught in its own clogged
craw and burned the lizard's
lungs.
It lifted and lunged but dropped
down heavily.
Then fumed and fought for air
and died a welcome death.

I viewed the venomous beast,
saw it lose its life.
Then went my way, leaving the
hidden hoard.
Taking only my trusted sword.
Not taking cursed treasure that
harms the heart and scars the
soul.
My duty became my desire.
I returned to my manor,
honoring my queen and kin.
Then lived my life telling none
of the hidden hoard,

59

But telling tales of truth that
warn of wandering ways.
When entering the utangard
maintain your innangard:
In troubled times many men and
women lose their way,
Lost to demons and dragons who
are secret and slow.
Even in today's times of peace
and plenty, many are taken by
traps they failed to find.
Prepare your place, watch the
woods, do not give up your
guard,
Even in a peaceful place trouble
can take security away.

John Sorensen

Heritage

"Tommeltot
Slikkepot
Langemand
Guldebrand
and Little Peter Spillemand.."

These are things you need to
know
Especially as you grow.
It is part of your heritage,
From your ancestors of past age.
It could be of Viking lore or
Maybe the Danes and more.
It could be of Irish or Welsh
descent
Or maybe the Scots are meant.
Englishmen are on the list,
Iceland should also not be
missed.
Holland is also listed there
With Norway and Greenland
showing up somewhere.

Elva Sorensen

*Note: The first 5 lines are the
names of the fingers, similar to
'This little piggie' in rhyme*

Voyage

Far and away I've been a while
Longing for that blessed isle.

Out to sea I've been sailing
The songs of home I hear calling

The honor of the voyage took me
The promise and the lure of
glory.

Fame and riches held and kept
me,
Sailing for my Gods and
country.

The code of Odin I would follow
Secure my place upon Valhalla.

On the waters I set course,
Pilaged, plundered with the
sword.
Many battles charged and fought
Grandeur to my name it brought.

But now my bones are old and
tired.
Needing warmth from the hearth
fire.

And time has come to return
To the land that I call home.

Jessica Brimley

I love cats

I love cats
I love baby tigers
They are so awesome
I love when they jump.

Unknown

Pokemon

I like to Battle with my Pokemon
My Pokemon is very strong.
He never gets along
With other Pokemons.
Charazard is my favorite one
He is a fire type and lots of fun.
There are many battles that he
has won.
Yes I like him a ton.

Tate Lewis

I know the bloke
I love this one because I know
the bloke who wrote it:

I killed a King, a Pope or two.
I've killed near everything,
except me and you. Our
collective dream, that still lives
too. To achieve it, we'll have to
kill some more, that's true.
When we're done we'll have
won or gone home. Either way,
I'm looking forward to the calm.

Stephen Templar

Amber Dream

With haste but not impatience a
lovely visitor came;
Of calm determined visage both
confident and wise.
Her golden hair a halo around
her perfect face;
Surpassed in beauty only by her
striking violet eyes.

Into my outstretched hand she
placed a small and aged box;
Burnished wood untarnished by
the touch of many fingers.
Inside an amber amulet with a
tiny golden chain;
And when I closed the box the
scent of ancient spices lingered.

She said to keep it safe, and
always within my reach;
To handle it with care so the
chain would not be broken.
I asked if I could wear it clasped
most carefully round my neck;
Surprisingly, she deferred to me
as the new owner of the token.

She instructed to deliver it as she
had done with me
To the next owner of the
necklace when the time was
fully come.
I queried how I would know to
whom the box should go

Quietly she assured me that I
would know the one.

I gazed upon the necklace,
perplexed by all that had
transpired
I carefully placed it in the box
and then fitfully fell asleep
The dream first came that night
and at least two nights thereafter
The third more vivid than the
rest but in each the same I see:

A young girl with golden hair
coming to the wharf at dawn
She wears a tiny amulet of
amber on a chain around her
neck
A gift from her dear mother as
she lay dying on her couch
With a gentle kiss and a whisper,
she was not coming back

She ducks behind casks of salted
fish so her father will not see her
Come to observe the trading
ships sailing in with the morning
tide
She watches the unloading of
cargo and hears the shouts of
sailors
Returning home or leaving when
their boat sails on the evening
tide.

Today there is a swarthy sailor
with tan skin and thick dark hair
He momentarily turns her way
and his visage is more than
memorable
She gasps with astonishment at
the sight of his striking violet
eyes
She then goes home
surreptitiously to complete her
morning chores

Her father is a tradesman and has
an office on the wharf
Traders come to purchase amber
with silver, gold and spice
When she returns to the wharf
delivering her father's mid-day
meal
The docks are filled with smoke
and men laboring to contain a
raging fire.

Robbed and beaten her father is
lying dead in a pool of his own
blood.
Shocked and stunned, blindly
she runs home, and collapses in
a heap
Opening her eyes she is
overcome with incalculable pain
within
She looks around for her father
then memory plunges her even
deeper

Now an orphan she trembles
with fright at what that may
portend,
Possessing nothing save the tiny
golden chain of amber round her
neck
She hires on for room and board
as a scullery maid at the local
inn
Receiving no wages her clothes
become tattered, and then
reduced to rags

She spends her days scrubbing
floors impossible to keep clean.
The inn is filled with nasty
odors, with acrid smoke blurring
the walls
She hauls wood, stokes the fire
and wipes down all the tables
Then at night she washes the
greasy dishes from the meals
served in the hall

One moonless night while
fetching wood, outside the
kitchen door
She is set upon by a group of
men, about them the sour smell
of ale
Brandished about, abused and
violated, at last she falls
unconscious
Upon awakening she pins up her
hair, and washes her face at the
well

When her body begins to swell
with child she is thrown into the
street,
Deemed a fallen woman not fit
to work in such a public and
notable place
Serving ale and food to sailors
with low morals and heavy
pockets.
Forced to beg, she sits at the
turnstile, where tolls are paid by
all that pass

At dusk a band of highwaymen
approaches with pounding
hooves,
She steps into the path with
outstretched arms and hopeful
gaze.
As one rider lashes with his
riding whip, she catches a
momentary glimpse
And even in the failing light she
recognizes, his striking violet
eyes.

Beaten, hopeless, starving and
cold, she lies upon the roadside;
Childbirth imminent, she slips
into unconsciousness.
Nigh to death, she is found by a
kindly man, and carried to the
nuns;
Delivered of her child she
quickly fades, and without
awaking passes

The golden chain with the
amulet is removed from round
her neck;
Safely kept, then given to her
young girl with the violet eyes.
Centuries pass and the necklace
graces many throats;
From one generation to the next,
it is the tie that binds.

Stirring from the dream I
reached beneath my pillow;
With trembling hands I removed
the necklace from the box;
I fastened it around my neck and
looked at my reflection;
The pale translucent amber set
off perfectly my golden locks.

I gazed in the mirror as I have
done so many times before;
Astonished as I realized the
significance of my reflection;
Staring at my violet eyes, I
pondered the instruction
To treat the amulet carefully so
the chain would not be broken.

Susan Sorensen

Kirsten Saga

'Twas on the rugged mountain ridge
And snow was on the ground.
Young Kirsten swore she'd hunting go
And never more was found.

"Beware the mount!" her mother said,
And begged her not to go.
"There's danger in its stony heart
And blood upon the snow!"

Her mother's words were naught to her.
The winter had been sore.
"I'll go!" she said. "I'll hunt the deer
And bring him to your door!"

Her bow and cloak upon her back,
Her father's sword in hand,
She climbed the snowy crags and slopes
That rose up from the land.

From high above her struggling path,
A trumpet echoed clear.
She raised her eyes and quicked her pace:
It was the mountain deer.

The trail was steep, its stones were cruel,
But still she forward pressed
Along the way her father'd gone
To reach the mountain crest.

The way led through the towering pines
whose branches, evergreen
Obscured in shadowed mystery
The place the stag had been.

Through drift and glade within the wood
The hoof prints led her on;
All day, all night, she stalked the deer
'Til it was almost dawn.

Then there, upon a craggy ridge,
His antlers like a crown,
The mountain deer defied her chase.
Her arrow brought him down!

But no! The stag reared up and roared.
Again she drew her bow--
His antlers struck the shaft aside--
There's blood upon the snow!

The wounded deer above her
stood;
Their blood together ran.
The stag gazed down at her,
aghast,
And then became a man.

He lifted her upon his arm,
Her wound beneath his hand.
"Beloved! Had I known 'twas
thee!
Dost thou know who I am?"

Her eyes, tho' dim and bathed
in mist,
She focused on his face.
"Oh, Father, have I passed
from earth?
How came you to this place?"

"My Kirsten, I was always
here.
This is my form and home.
Thy mother was my own true
love,
But here she would not come."

She drew another rasping
breath;
Her blood was cold as stone.
"If I'm to die upon the mount,
Then she will be alone."

"Her loneliness I cannot
change;
Her grief I cannot stave,
But as my child, my blood, my
kin,
Thy life I can save."

"I will not see my mother
starve,
Tho' I, as deer, might live."
"If thou with me would stay,"
he said,
"My treasure I will give!"

She brought the gold to her
mother's door
And laid it on the ground.
Brave Kirsten did a-hunting go
And never more was found.

Lynn Sorensen

66

The Very Hungry Níðhöggr

In the light of the dawn of the tree
Lay an egg on the Náströnd in Hel
And beneath one of Yggdrasil's three
Did the serpent-like "malice-Strike"
dwell.

As he hatched in the rays of the morn,
He did have his first urges to feed,
And the dragon Hvergelmir-born
On the Shore of the Corpses craved greed.

On the day of his birth he ate thief
For the goods they in borrowing stole,
And still hungering swallowed two cheats
For their robb'ry of honesty cold,

Sucked three plagiarists dry of their blood
For their forgery of Kvasir's Meade,
And while searching for more lawless curd,
Picked four charlatans out of his teeth.

As five corpulent gluttons went down,
Níðhöggr realized that he hungered still.
So he broadened his scope of the crowd,

In the hopes that his stomach he'd fill.

He ate:
Racketeers, mountebanks, swindlers, cons,
Murderers, flimflammers, perjurers, frauds,
Hustlers, slaughterers, terrorists, shams,
Manslayers, shoplifters, heretics, and
Níðhöggr had eaten more than he could stand.

So seeking new diets he started to climb
And broaden his diet beyond Niflheim.
He chewed and he chewed at the root of the tree
Until Yggdrasil fell and the world ceased to be.

He rested in darkness – this purpose fulfilled –
As gods battled monsters and millions were killed.
He rose from his slumber on wings of the dead
To herald the New World, or so it was said…

Skye Caden

67

The Viking

Once there was a viking with his
axe and shield.
Sitting on a log looking for his
filthy hog.
He sat for a moment and had an
idea.
I think I'll throw my axe at a target.
So he grabbed his axe and … what?
Where is the target?
Oh! My shield will do it.
So he was staring at the target and
at that split second
the axe went flying until his brother
came around the
corner and crack, the axe went right
through his skull.
The end. Or is it?

So, the Viking stared at his hog.
Then he had another idea.
He grabbed his hog and the axe tied
the axe to a tree.
He grabbed his hog and he threw
his hog.

Unknown

The Brave Viking

The viking was baking his hen
and he went far and far.
He saw a fox chasing a rabbit
and the fox caught the rabbit.
The viking went to get the
rabbit and he cooked it.
The End.

Unknown

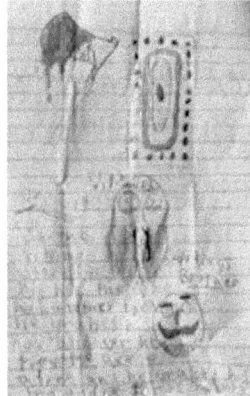

More than Everything

Beware, young things, and old ones too! There are strange creatures about. These may seem only imagined when you catch them from the corner of your eye. But they are there, lurking. Just waiting for your guard to drop and your attention to wane. For this life is but illusion and when we stop believing we pass out of it back to the place where we are from.

The nature of our kind is that we are the powerful ones. Thor, Odin, Freya and Loki are only the names that you know. Many of us walk among you. We who are from the dark or from the light. We wear a skin that looks like yours. We squeeze into these limited containers to experience the loss of power. How can we learn if a thought brings our every desire to our hand? How can we love if we know nothing of loss and sacrifice? How can we care if we have never needed to be cared for and perhaps, just perhaps, gone without?

You see, we are all Gods. Some of us will be defined by the great deeds we do and some will be forged into a sharp and strong axe. The trials we face were agreed upon before we chose to come. We knew the path, and knew we would forget that we knew once we entered this mortal existence.

Finding the "meaning of life" is a pointless exercise. LIFE is the meaning of life. Live it. Learn from it. Being the object of abuse or neglect was the door to who you are, or who you could be, by the time you're done walking this journey. Be not a Victim! Be a student.

As for those things lurking about, they are there to feed on your fears, pain, loneliness and suffering. They are drowned by joy, love, laughter and fun. Drown them. Do not listen to their poking, prodding whispers that take you down the path where you become food for them. Instead, crush their bones as the stairs you need to move to the next level. Though my tale does not follow the hero's journey, You will follow the heroes journey. Be the hero in your own life! Love, learn, choose and act to learn what you chose to learn, to fulfill the duty you accepted, and to become more than everything.

69

Monsters

A Saga of Naga

Perhaps the monsters had always lain
Just beneath the skin
Mind and body rent in twain
Bloody battle deep within

Evil creatures screech and roar
Clawing, gnashing
Shook to the core

Twisted faces grinning out
Cloaked in darkness
Yell and shout

And all these creatures
Scaring me
Ugly features
Cannot flee

The hateful faces
Hurt my soul
Damaging phrases
Pushing me into a hole

Ariane Millet

The humans are our friend
With every card we play,
Around each every bend
And everything we say.

But now we are in war
Cause they made a little flaw,
There's much we're fight for
They have an enfeild paw.

This war has took a turn
We had a little stomp,
They're hiding in the fern
But they know we're in the swamp.

The humans are now winning
I guess that we were wrong,
Cause now the world is spinning
But we can still stand strong.

Now the war is won
Though many blood was spilt I'd say
Without the human gun
We rose to save the day

And in the end
These Naga
O, my friend
I put into my saga

Sawyer Brimley

An Unfortunate Viking Voyage

Once in a Viking village
There lived Toke, Sten and
Frode
Searching for adventure
Off in their ship they rode

They sailed for nine days and
nights
And on the tenth day at sea
Being hungry and tired
An island they did see

But before they could get there
A sea monster attacked
The men tried to sail away
But it was way too fast

The monster started crushing
Their ship to tiny shreds
So the three men swam for shore
Longing for their beds

When they set foot upon the land
They took a look around
There was a big pile of rocks
And trees tall and round

Toke went to look in the trees
And Sten went to the rocks
Frode went to look for some
food
And brought back a small ox

"There is a hole here!" cried
Sten
A deep hole in the rocks
That the three men walked into
As they ate that small ox

Soon they came to a large cave
With lots of jewels in it
Now they had to get off this
island
And this trio could not quit it

Raegan Brimley

71

The Donkey

Once upon a time
In a kingdom far away
Lived a farmer and his donkey
Munching on some hay

The farmer's name was William
But people called him Bill
The donkey was called
Quickstep
But his mama named him Gill

Suddenly one morning
Gill began to speak
Not in animal language
But how we people greet

"The same old things keep
happenin'
Here on this old farm
Goin' on adventures
Is the thing that brings me
charm."

"What's happened to you
Quickstep"
Exclaimed a startled Bill
"My name ain't Quickstep" He
replied.
"You should call me Gill."

Poor William stood speechless
Not knowing what to do
If your donkey's started talking
I bet that you would too

Neither knew what's happened
Whether spell or curse
Neither of them could decide
For better or for worse

But Bill listened to Gill
They packed then started off
Seeking some adventure
Sleeping inside lofts.

They came upon a troll
With stinky monster breath
Next they found a dragon
Feared above the rest

And though they found
adventure
Neither was happy
So they returned home
To their fields so grassy

The moral of the story
Listen as you read
That what you think you want
Isn't always what you need.

Karleigh Brimley

Fantasy Story Lines

Once upon a Long time ago
in a galaxy far, far away
There once lived a hobbit
Eating his curds and whey

He sat atop a tall stone wall
And ate his curds and whey
He sat upon the tall stone wall
And ate the day away

He sat upon this tall stone wall
Overlooking the village green
He sat atop the tall stone wall
Where all the town could be seen

He watched the girl run up the
hill
Following her brother
While they gathered from the
well
Some water for their mother

There was an egg
That sat by him
With two legs
Who talked to him

There was a stalk
Of magic beans
And on the top
Could not be seen

Beyond the mountains
It reached the clouds
Above the fountain
And very loud

Now there was a giant foot
Reaching down the giant stalk
Reaching down it really could
reaching down 'til it could walk

There was a leg
And then an arm
A giant leg
That would cause harm

The neck appeared
And then the head
A giant ear
And then the rest

And then his voice
Echoing like thunder
Said this mans choice
Was pillage and plunder

I'll eat him up
And return
And hurry up
With golden urn

He took my gold
He took my food
I'm very old
But still eat stew

I'll take him too
And chop him up
Put him in stew
And gobble up

And as the halfling
Jumped off the wall
The egg named Humpty
Began to fall

As he fell
There was a shout
Now broken shell
Yelled help me out

The egg turned brown
In the mud
And hit the ground
With a thud

He saw the horses
He heard the men
But they couldn't put Humpty
Together again

The yellow ooze
Began to leak
By the canoes
Into the creek

And aroused
A tiny squeak
There was a mouse
And very weak

That little mouse
And then another
And then a third
But still no mother

The little mice
Ran past them
Running from
The giant thumb

The giant came
And he followed
The tall and thin
But handsome fellow

The lad ran past
Andy ran too
Before they got squished
By a giant shoe

The giant reached
To grab them all
And then he stumbled
And started to fall

The giant sneezed
And blew them down
And they flew
Through the town

The houses blurred
As they got blown
But they still heard
The thud and groan

The giant fell
And crushed some houses
He smashed the bell
And almost the mouses

They heard a cry
From the mice
Still on the fly
But that was nice

No mouse was squished
And nor were they
And they had all
Survived that day

74

The boy ran home
And so did some others
The knights went home
But the mice had no mother

They were alone
And lived off of scraps
They had no home
But still took some naps

They were taken in
On that day
By the hafling
To seep in warm hay

They stayed with each other
After all that day
They were kind to one another
And they all ate curds and whey

Sawyer Brimley

Chapter 7 – 2020, Covid-19, and 2021

Due to the Covid-19 pandemic, the family did not meet for the reunion in 2020.
Our beloved mother underwent many health scares in 2020, and other members of the family suffered severe health issues.

Of note:
Mom was in the hospital for several days a month with one thing or another. She grew weaker each day.

John Sorensen fell and severely concussed his head. He nearly died in a parking lot, while Julie did CPR shouting at him not to leave her.

Morgan Templar had Covid in February 2020 before anyone know how to treat it; she had 5-point pneumonia, sepsis, and Sars Cov-2 virus. She was hospitalized, spending 5 days on a ventilator. Stephen spent every day at her side, battling Covid himself, but insisting that Morgan stay with him.

Others had challenges and issues. It was a year of separation. By Christmas we had learned to use Zoom and joined together from the various states.

We did gather in 2021, knowing it was very likely the last year of Elva Sorensen's life.

We knew her as Mom, My Mother, Grandma, Great-Grandma, and Great-Great Grandma.

2021 was Mom's last reunion.

More people than any other year made the effort to convene from around the country to celebrate our family heritage one last time with Grandma. We spoke and sang many poems of love and recognition of our mortality. Nobody collected the poems – it was not the primary thing on our minds. We were able to gather a few later, although there are many more that are missing.

On the week we would have celebrated her birthday in October 2021, we gathered for remembrance. We buried Mom with memories of love and joy. The kids played "The Grandma Game" one last time in her living room to distribute her many collections: Mr. Potato Head dolls, Beanie-Babies, and pop-up books. Everyone took something home to remember her.

Poems of 2021 – Star Wars

Mom's Poem for The Reunion

Another year come and gone,
So let's see what we've
accomplished here.
A year older, that's for sure
But I'm sure there's got to be
more.
We've grown taller, wider, richer
and poorer, But, oh well, we've
been happy and content.
My kids have grown smarter and
bigger.
The grandkids have got their
own problems now,
And I can just enjoy their
mistakes and Don't have to have
answers.
Their folks have that
opportunity.
I'm the old folk now,
And don't I know it: can't see,
hear or walk.
Well, I can still smell.
I don't have to worry about
getting
Thin or fat, or which bill to pay
And what to fix to eat,
Or drive to get things done.

It's too late for that.
I'm happy and content to just sit
here.
I think what to write and
If I don't write quick enough
I've forgot The thought.
And I can't see to read what I've
wrote,
So I leave it at that.

Elva Sorensen 2021

For Julie on our 50th Wedding Anniversary

It has been fifty years,
But it seems to me,
That the time has been shorter,
Than I thought it would be.

There has been easy and hard,
As we went on our way,
But the hard always faded,
And the good always stayed.

When I was frightened,
With no place to hide,
You took my hand,
You walked by my side.

When I felt strong,
And walked steadily,
You walked by my side,
Stronger than me.

Your kindness,
Your smile,
Your beautiful eyes,
Your long flowing hair,
 Your first snow surprise,

Your beautiful voice,
Your beautiful face,
Your soft tender touch,
Your eternal grace,

Have all been my gift,
My blessing to share,
Have always been mine,
Have always been there.

Now it has been fifty years,
Together we stand,
As we start fifty more,
As we walk hand in hand.

John Sorensen April 2021

Horses

I like horses
I like riding them
I like their color
They are pretty

And I like Rainbows
And Butterflies and
Bunnies and
Dolphins and
Fairies – the way they fly

And toys. They make me feel
Good.

Amilia

Forever Friends

We were three
The poet, the songstress, and me
Childhood friends, determined,
To remain so - for forever.

A coin was cast into the stream
And each a promise made
To share the journey faithfully
Wherever it might lead

Childhood dreams like fairy dust
Gave flight to fancy free
Castles built and mountains
scaled
With fearlessness and joy

Progression of maturity
Narrowed thoughts of possibility
Youthful beings and feeble
wings,
Rejected the velocity

Realities of mortality
Replaced ambitious thoughts
With the dust at last depleted
The vow was faded, then forgot

Will we chart the course anew?
Soar with strengthened wings to
flight?
The coin awakened, the bonds
renewed,
When veil and mist have
Given way to farther sight?

Perhaps then to be forever three
The poet, the songstress, and me

Susan Sorensen

Family

Video games are super fun
But sometimes I'm just done.
You can do things like look at
the sun,

My family makes me proud,
but sometimes they're just loud.
So, I'll go outside to find a bead
But sometimes I'll just read.

But at the end of the day
Family is the way.

JuliAnne

Hoardings

(A temporary board fence
placed around a building
being erected or repaired.
--Merriam-Webster)

Old books reread to tatters and
old
Magazines stacked among
metaphors
And places we'll never go.

Albums pressed with places and
people
We've been and won't be again
Faded dim and dusting.

Recipes we made and remade
and
Replayed and put in a box and
Forgot to save the steps.

Pails of rusty nails waiting
For lost hammers and old lumber
We'll need when things fall
apart.

Stamps and stones and shiny
things in
Empty vases filled with the
smell of
Ashes and asters and first
gardenias.

All the important things we can't
Throw away like fragments of
memory
And pieces of string too small to
use

Lynn Sorensen

82

Chapter 8 – 2022 Waterpark

Who Told Thee

Who told thee
This is all there would be
A prolonged journey
A future you'd never imagine;

How will we know
When we come to the shore
And pause, one foot in the water.
Who told thee It was over.

Lynn Sorensen

Valdez

A night in sunshine
Water rushing down Shear cliffs
Welcoming sea birds

Rhea Cragun

Dinosaurs

I'm a mothasaurus that eats meat
Fish are my favorite treat
I'll snack on anything
I mostly eat in summer and
spring
And you are hiding from me
You'd better be able to swim in
the sea.

Noah (read by Mary)

The night of wind

At night when it is dark and still
and everyone is sleeping
I lie quietly on my bed and listen
for the wind.
I cannot hear it yet. It is hiding
in the mountains.
But soon it will come tearing
down swift and loud and
whining.
I hear it first as it approaches,
like a mutter from afar,
With baited breath I wait as it
grows from groan to roar.
Engulfs the house with sound
like a freight train approaching.
Then it passes reluctantly to
dwindle in the desert.
This first onslaught of the night
of wind, is not the end, I know.
Succeeding doth grow grander
still and I pray that it will stop.
Wind, like giant waves of water,
assaults my bedroom window
Until the morning sun appears
upon the mountain top.
Wind is not so scary in the light
when all the leaves are quaking,
But in the night, with darkness
thick, I imagine tree limbs
breaking.

Susan Sorensen

Summer fun

"Just go outside," our mom
exclaims. Summer plans no
more profane. We rush to meet
the world at large. Shodden feet
and stick fomage. Warm sun,
warm fun and smiles to match.
Dry throat, dry mouth and itchies
to match.

"We Thirst!" we yell. "Can we
come in?" "No, you may not.
There's too much din." Running,
seeking, a drop to quench. There,
a hose, beside a bench. Hot
rubber, hot tin, a smell sublime.
Anxious throats stand in line.
Pushers push to be near, wiser
ones hang to the rear.
To be the first is hard to beat,
except of course for summer
heat.

Here it comes, here we go.
Boiling current bursts and flows.
Steaming acrid welcome wet.
We bear the brunt, our thirst is
met. Bellies sloshing eager lips,
poling elbows, bumping hips.
Fresh and full, forgotten needs.
Off we run into the trees.

Aaron Davis

Warm Water

I waited at the table for the
waiter to arrive.
He asked me what I wanted.
"Water," I replied.
"What else can I get you?" the
waiter asked of me. "You must
want more than water. What else
can I bring?"
"I just want some water, water's
what I want. If you bring me
water, just make sure it's warm."
"Wait, you want warm water?"
the waiter asked in surprise.
"Well, the water's not for me.
It's for Walter," I replied.
"So Walter wants warm water?"
the waiter was bemused.
"Who is Walter? And where is
he?"
"He will be here soon."
He walked away bewildered and
brought back a big tall glass.
From my waistband satchel, I
pulled out a plastic bag.
The waiter stared in wonder. I
smiled then I gave a wink. Then
poured in the warm water and
gave my fish a drink.

Jessica Brimley

We breath water

They came from the bay
Rolling in with the tide
On a late summer day at the end
of July

Some people saw strangers
lurking near the woods
And horses sans rangers with
inverted hooves.

They stayed by the water to lure
children in
Then commenced with the
slaughter and ripped through the
skin.

With teeth sharp like pins
Their needle like nails
They swam with their fins and
Their sleek shiny tails.

From deep ocean sands and
They had to vacate.
For the oil began to sink and
suffocate.

The fish were no more
They sickened and died.
So the Kelpies sought shore and
that story is why
The kids now adays must be
careful around
Each wet, wavy place where
they can't touch the ground.

Find sea tangled hair to spot
these foul creatures
Survivors prepare to lose all
their fingers.

Skye Caden

Wet Noses

Wet noses, playful paws
Lots of energy, small claws
Chasing through the grass,
Racing, pacing,
I feel like running forever,
but suddenly my pace stops all
together.
Something catches my eye
Where did it come from?
Where? Why?
It feels very damp. And the
temperature's just right. It feels
so good, my heart is tipping,
light.
I think I remember what it's
called.
Wh, wha, water. Not a boring
name at all.
It's tickling my nose from a
gorgeous garden hose.
I catch your attention as I bound
on my feet
Looks like someone has a treat.
Some people say, I'm only a pet
But for a dog, this is as good as
it can get.

Eva (read by Mary)

85

History of Water

The history of water is the
history of the west
The faithful moved by the
prophets behest.
From the green of Denmark's far
land to the grey clay and sand.
Called a mere trickle at home,
In this land, a creek.
For the brave or the fool, not for
the meek.
Try it here on the Muddy, then
move south a mile.
Put faith to the test, sanctified by
the trial.
Dig trenches, dig holes. Build
houses, cut trees
Marry, have babies, die of
disease.
Look to the water, the flow of
the creek.
Will crops grow or just salt at
your feet?
Plant mulberries, speargrass,
along every ditch
Maybe, think how years later
which
Of your progeny, the barefoot
young thing,
Would pick the small stalks in
early spring.
Would play in the rag week and
play in salt grass,
Would know only desert, and not
your green past.
Who would build jigsaw puzzles
in dried cracking clay,
Would swim with tadpoles on a
hot summer day.
Who would not stay in that place
With its too little water and vast
open space.
But history and longing will pull
her back
To the smell of the willow and
the grey dusty track.
To the Swell, the Sinbad, the
Muddy Creek, to the towns of
her childhood where today I
speak,
Of a beauty she dissed in youth's
naïve mind
That now she comes eager and
grateful to find.
The history of water, the history
of place.
My history of beauty, connection
and grace.

Mary Mealing

A Caustic Attack

What goblins desire
Attack villages and farms
Terror spreading beasts,
evil raiders stealing land
retreat to caves at daybreak

Josh Sorensen

Water

Flowing, rushing down the
stream
Water, water pulling me.
Little boat that bobs and dips
All sides splashing, water drips
Fish are jumping in the waves
Paddling on sunny days
Oops, a little far we've flipped
Now our little boat has tipped.
Swimming to the surface now
Laughing, giggling, at just how
Clumsily we fell right in.
Good thing we know how to
swim.

Karleigh Brimley

Games

Sorry, I can't reach it
I wait for many hours, I'm bored
I put my swimsuit on
I sing a song I
I cant reach the top shelf
So I guess we'll play another
game

Millie

Water Rushing

Water rushing down my front
Shooting sharp spikes of pain
here and there
Standing on a stool in front of
the sink
Water overflowing
Seeps under the door and under
the stove
Picking up electricity that burns
and stabs
Incoherent emotion of water
hurting
Tears running down my cheeks
Too acidic leaving burn trails
where they touch
My own bioelectric field
changing
Putting out lightbulbs as I walk
by
Draining batteries when my
emotions flare
(the energy has to come from
somewhere)
Making myself shower, because,
ick
But wishing it could be dry
Water rushing down my front

Morgan Templar

87

Rain on her hair

In a land far, far away with
mountain peaks so high
A castle stands within a city
With towers that scrape the sky.

A frantic maid is searching
round for something that's not
there.
The only princess, not in sight,
The only royal heir.

Through glade and glen, cross
narrow streams, on sturdy horse
she rode. Golden hair blowing in
the wind, she entered the secret
grove.

Dismount, fixing her auburn
skirts, when blowing through the
trees,
The smell of rain is in the air
Rocks crunch beneath her feet.

Her love is waiting there for her,
A man of wolves and wood.
An outcast to the city men
Since his childhood.

She ran to him with arms
outstretched, embraced him in a
hug. He kissed her forehead,
spun her around, "I've missed
you long, my love."

The pouring started, drenching
them. They kissed and said
goodbye. Pulled apart once
again, they both had tears to cry.

The princess rode her horse back
home and snuck into her room.
Leaving trails of water across the
floor, she went to sleep in
gloom.

Oblivious to the mess she made
and forgetting to change her
gown,
While she slept her handmade
found this and ran to tell the
crown.

Early in the morning she rose
and found the guards outside her
door.
She climbed out the window and
down the vine, as she had done
before.

She ran out into the city with a
dark hood on her head, Past the
sleeping sentries and to the dark
grove she fled.

She told her love what happened.
"I can't see you anymore. I don't
think that I was followed, but
this love cannot endure."

"Run away with me," he said.
But not a moment later, The
king and his soldiers stormed
into the
grove. The king was yelling,
"Traitor!"

They were taken to the city, as
they fought and screamed.
And as they got to the city
square, they saw the guillotine.

He was dragged to his
impending doom and his head
was locked in place.
His eyes looked into hers with
love and sorrow filled his face.

As the blade fell to the ground,
and grieving in despair,
The princess took her final
breath. Her heart beyond
repair.

Raegan Brimley

Valdez

A night in sunshine
Water rushing down sheer cliffs
Welcoming sea birds

Rhea Cragun

The Raven's way

I think I found it
It was rest upon a raven's wing
Passed away the swaying creek
I set myself next to the body
And I let the blood and cold
pour, it's frigid.
I know it. Encased in blood, the
smell bathed the true me in
sweat
It grew in my lungs
It hurt, it was real
The currents dug deeper as I
caved
It tends to leave the situation
scar every tissue in me
Moulded into something wrong
The meaning of life was never a
purpose, it's acceptance
The realization that we don't
need a reason. Why cut strings
stitched with time and
convention. She spun words with
quiet carelessness, through
blood, through death. Til that is
simply me because even through
a thread we live.

Ariane Millet

Memory

The wind is warm upon my face.
The scent of salt, sand and
juniper embrace.
It softens the bruises of
yesteryear.
Forgotten lifted memories that
felt like the current tears.
The fire ants move mountains.
The boulders perched on a cliff.
The trout stand still.
As I listen to the locusts ask
permission to pass, the following
time allows me to heal.
I'm haunted not by ghosts and
ghouls under bridges and
wooden roads, after all my aunts
taught me how to fight off those.
I'm haunted by neighbour dads
and families near and far. They
sneak around the rocks like
rivers stealing motion and sick
like flight all a blur of pain and
fright.
Generational trauma acts like
poison, healing feels like
erosion, but nothing ever goes
away.
It just changes. We just change.
But hopefully the sun shines
along the way.

Autumn Mohr

The Evil

The birds made whistles and
clumps, but when the night fell,
all was still, for all creatures
feared the evil.
It lurks quite far in the deep all
who see it tremble and weep.
Its tentacles, like long black
cords, defeated all the spears and
swords.
None have lived who have ever
seen, its bird-like beak of darkest
green.
It reaches out every night and
drags in all that's in sight.
That's why they teach, and all
learn, that all who face it never
return.
Its power grows stronger every
hour, with every bite of each
thing it devours.
Until the warrior of the light
stepped forward to face it in the
night.
He was never seen ever again.
He had the world of men to save
and took the beast with him to
the grave.

Sawyer Brimley

Fleas

Fleas need something to live one. They don't have enough fleas for their fleas to live on. When an "Oocon?" gets bitten, he feeds the flea to his brother. So you might say, indirectly, they are eating each other.

Next the silky haired warbling yark swings by its beak all night. He sings in the dark. If you were to see it in the dark of the dark, the silky haired yark would be quite a sight. But the yark never sings in the light of the day. It never has time to eat, sleep, sing or play. It spends the whole day combing its hair that gets tangled in the night while it's swinging.

Here is the long legged loper. Who likes to have fun. The way that it does it is to run, run, run, run. It runs the whole night and runs the whole day. The long legged loper is always running away.
But, the long legged loper is always right here, even when it's been running all year. Because the long legged loper is so tiny, so small, it runs its whole life and goes nowhere at all.

Now the big footed short legged long-walking cray has been walking to town for years, so they say. He starts early each morning at the first morning's light. Goes exactly halfway and stops for the night. He does exactly the same thing every single day. He starts first in the morning and goes halfway.
So it looks like the cray will get to town never. Because going halfway each day will take him forever. But if you ask him about it he won't care. He'll just smile and say, I'm half way there.

The two digit binary yount does what it loves. But what it loves is to count. It counts the hairs on your head and the ears on your pup. It counts up and down and it counts down and up.
It counts bugs flying by and birds flying away. Then it counts the times it has counted today. But with only two fingers, it counts in base 2, so it has to count faster than we do.

Look down in the water. Look down deep. There's an air-breathing critter that goes down there to sleep. No one knows what it looks like because no one is there when it wakes up and comes up for air. So if you happen to see it, you'll earn some fame. Because you'll be the one that gets to give it its name.

The great toothed snapper gives me the jitters. Cuz the great toothed snapper is the meanest of critters.
So we watch it all night and we watch it all day. But sometime last night, I'm sorry to say, it snatched up its watcher and sneaked right away. So I can't show you the snapper and the reason is because we don't know where it's at.

I'm sorry to say that I can't show you more, because this day is over. That's the end of our tour.

I hope you have learned that if you take the chance, you will learn more than you would with just a quick glance. You can be sure, just like you learned here, when you understand more, you have less to fear.

Anyplace in the world you happen to go, you will always find something that you don't know. It's a great big world, and you have seen a small part. You can't know it all, but you can make a good start.
So put down your gadget with touch screen or key, take a deep breath, a big step and get out there to see.

Thank you for coming and spending the day. I hope you had fun before you went on your way. You have seen lots of things you can only see here. You'll see many more when you come back next year.

John Sorensen

Chapter 9 – 2023 Halloween

Remainders

A pile of papers was sent to me.
To transcribe here for you to read.
Some have names and others naught
Some are joyful, others fraught
With pain and sorrow belted out
In tearful songs or with a shout.

Yet, poems were written, handed in
And I am typing them again.
As tribute to the family's tries,
I place them here to be no lies.

I know not who wrote or spoke some of these poems.
If remembered or one of yours, please make it known.

Putting this legacy into a book
Letting friends and strangers have a look
Into the workings of our minds
Worked into these many lines.

It's bravery to tell the truth
For real life is reflected by age or youth
To put our stories together here
And release them to the world now without fear.

I have been away for many years.
Missed lots of fun and lots of tears.
The legacy that I pass through
Will scatter, gather and continue

For though we're near or far away
The turn of phrase, the rhyme, the day
Will catch our ear and spark a thought
That may end up here, likely or not.

Morgan Templar

Cryptic Foreshadowing

It's been an interesting week.
I've seen some unexpected
things.

The tides are turning, the winds
are shifting, the pressure's
increasing.

Clearly, it has begun, that cannot
be missed. But, to the last, we'll
try our best to pretend it isn't so.

From Magic to Tech, the
strangeness is all around. The
sands are shifting, the world is
burning, and we say it isn't so.

Things that have been silent are
among us once again. Others,
who would consume us, ceased
to be and fell away.

As the clock keeps ticking and
the world keeps shifting, soon
we'll all be in it.
That's not good, but we must if
what is to come may be.

Eat, Drink, be Merry. Be Aware,
Be Prepared.

What comes next may surprise
you. If it does, then you missed
it. Don't fret about what's after,
it matters not until it's done.

Parabellum is the word,
Stella Umbra is where they hide.
Navis Longa is how we beat
them.
Victoria Unum is not our guy.

Whatever you see, you hear, you
do…
Be ready for the unexpected;
even friends will turn on you.

See you on the other side, I
hope. If not, it's been some fun.
Try not to die too soon, try not to
linger on.

If this note strikes you as
confusing,
Read it again, some six years on.
I'll see you then, I'll be just as
strange, we'll be closer, but
we'll carry on.

Stephen Templar

A Haunting With No Wanting

In eerie castles dreary and dark,
Where haunting tales begin to
embark. Three frightful
creatures, tales renowned,
Dracula, Frankenstein and the
Raven crowned.

Bram Stoker's count,
bloodthirsty and bold, Dracula's
story, centuries old. His fangs
glisten, his ape unfurled,
Beware, young souls, of the
vampire world.

Mary Shelley's creation, stitched
with might. Frankenstein's
monster born in the night. Bolts
through his neck, a fearsome
site. Monstrous whispers beneath
the pale moonlight.

Edgar Allan Poe's Raven,
perched above. A harbinger of
sorrow and lost love. Its
mournful cry fills the chilling
air. A dark omen that none can
bear.

Dracula rises from his coffin's
embrace. Bat wings flutter, a
nightmare's chase. He seeks the
blood of the living, beware. As
he prowls through the mist with
a menacing stare.

Frankenstein's creature, stitched
with despair. Trapped in a world
with nobody to care. He longs
for acceptance, a place to
belong, buts his monstrous
visage frightens all along.

The Raven's shadow spread
sings of dread, Its croaking voice
echoes, filling heads.
"Nevermore!" it cries, with
ghostly glee, Bringing dread to
all who dare to see.

These classic horror converge
tonight. In this haunting tale, a
spine-chilling plight. Dracula,
Frankenstein, and the Raven's
dread, Creating fear that fills
every thread.

So gather close, little ones, with
hearts strong. As the legends of
darkness linger long. For in these
tales, lessons unfold. Courage
and Kindness, a tale worth being
told.

Unknown

My Broken Arm

As I was going up and down
I did not have a frown
Then suddenly I fell down
It took an hour and a half to get
where I needed to be
It was plain to see
That fingers were touching my
wrist
And the doctor said jump at your
won risk
As he popped it back in place
Just to get a brace

I was in pain for three more days
Then I had to wear a cst for more
than 3 weeks.

As the daughter speaks to me
As she cuts my cast off
I immediately wanted to jump up
and down
On my trampoline
But it wasn't before long that I
scraped my know.

Susan Davis

Bubbles in the Pond

In the cool of midnight:
Slow concatenation of sludge
and sound.
A slump in the stillness.
Soft footsteps through the
trees.
Sodden slither along the
bottom.
Stirring of dead leaves and
ancient sediment.
Fearful and laughing.
Hate-full and hungry.
Invisible – peering up
Through grey viscosity.
Apparent –Peering down
Through green Opacity.
Shadow drawn to shadows.
Moonlit fancies cast
Like skipping stones
Across the muddy water.
Dark ripple of tendon and
tentacle –
Like tangled moss
Within the turbid depth.
Hands placed on the face of
the water—
In the cool of midnight
We do not see the
Bubbles in the Pond.

Lynn Sorensen

Ghosts are Just Lonely

People think they haunt
And act all scary and mean
But ghosts are not so gaunt
They don't try to make you
scream

They've been misunderstood
Ghosts aren't selfish brutes
What's underneath their hoods
Is really all too cute

Their simple floating forms
Are adorable little shapes
They have a tiny door
And two eyes to make a face

On the outside a ghost might
look
Like a person in cloak to their
jaw
But this appearance is mistook
For they're more like little blobs

The human figure is disguise
It's really just pretend
To look normal to human eyes
And try to get a friend

They might inhabit towns
Or hide within your houses
But the only reason they frown
Is they're lonelier than a mouse
is

So next time you see a ghost
Ask them to show themselves
They'll be your best ever host
And a friend like no one else.

Sawyer Brimley

Molasses

I feel like trash
And I have a bad rash,
I was just putting on my glasses
When came a big wave of
molasses,

It was hard to breathe
And I could not see
Because my glasses fell off
And I forgot to put water in the
trough.

I was stuck for three days.
And there weren't many ways to
get out.
It wasn't very long before death
arrived.

Amelia Davis

97

Halloween at Dr. Seuss' House by the Sea

In the darkest night, when the moon is bright,. Where shadows dance and creatures take flight. I'll tell you a tale, oh, listen with care, of bats, toads, ghosts, witches, goblins and a narwhal rare!

High up in the sky, bats flit and sway, With leather wings, they glide and play. Their beady eyes gleam, teeth sharp as a knife, as they swoop and dive through the eerie night.

Down in the swamp, where toads make their home. Their croaky chorus gives you a chill to the bone. Their warts and bumps make them quite scary. But they hop and splash, never too wary.

Ghost cone floating, their forms a blur, With chains that clank and whispers that slur, They moan and groan, so ethereal and pale, Spooky apparitions, haunting every trail.

Witches cackle, their cauldrons a-brew, With potions and spells, they conjure and do. Pointy hats and broomsticks. Oh what a sight, As they fly through the night, causing fright.

Goblins creep, sneaky and sly, With mischievous grins, they catch your eye. They hide in shadows, ready to pounce, Playing tricks and pranks at every ounce.

But amidst this frightful, eerie night, A narwhal appears, shining so bright. With its spiralling tusk, long and grand, It brings a touch of magic to this haunted land.

The narwhal swims with grace and poised. In ghostly waters, it makes no noise. Its presence a wonder, mystical and rare. A beacon of hope in this frightful affair.

So beware, little ones, as the night grows dark. With bats, toads, ghosts, witches, and goblins that bark. But remember the narwhal, brave and true. And let its magic guide and protect you.

For in this spooky world where fears take flight, Courage and kindness will shine the brightest light. Embrace the magic, let your imagination soar, And may you find joy in the scares and more!

Unknown

98

I heard him breathe

I heard him breathe again.
Drawing on, dripping down the
lengths of…however long it's
been. A silent, chord-less howl.

I could hear his smile drip. Or
whatever it is, the stationary
impersonation of a crescent.

I'm sat. Like a secret. As my
tension stings against my ribcage
and its accessories, I swallowed
too big.

The wood creaks.

Liquid hits the ground like few
words spoken.

I can almost hear how the ooze
bleeds out, in chunks…in
splatters…
Like a silent conversation.
Chatting with the floorboards.

He weeps…

In tears of something inky.

A toothless grin seeps and
nostrils bleed.

I can hear his bones creak
His limbs hung high in
awkward, sharp, angles.
Holding himself spider-like.

Seconds like hours.
Feeling out in this constant
checkmate.
Begging and bending in demise.
A coin toss with two heads,
waiting for the thumbnail to
flick.

And something moves.
A creak.
A splatter.
A dip in the wood too close for
comfort.

And windpipes aching and
bubbling through the endless
stream of thick black, sliding
down the sides of
…well…whatever time it is.

In days, in weeks, and in the
scheme of things, all seconds.

All seconds or all hours. All
concepts of something linear,
something tangible, molded and
rotted in the sludge that is our
space.

I this shadows lace, spun and
manipulated around me too tight
to breathe. This waiting, this
silence, this writhing worm, this
prey I've become…I feel the
force of something…

…I feel gravity in the
floorboards.

I feel vision on my skin.
I feel the bubble on my tongue…
I feel flesh inches from my own.
I feel the widows patience peak.

I heard him breath again.
And I felt the weight of it…

Ariane Millet

Lightning Bug or Firefly

What is the difference between a
lightning bug and a firefly?
I asked the man next door.

He looked at me with uncertainty,
And said he wasn't sure.

So, I looked it up on the Internet,
Like everybody does.

And the Internet guys, who never
lie,
Told me what it 'wuzz.'

It seems if you are from the West,
And talk with a Western twang.

Just at dusk when a bug lights up,
A firefly is its name.

But if you are from the south,
And have that Southern drawl.

Then at evening time when all is
fine,
It's a lightning bug, y'all.

I sat on the porch watching the
lightning bugs,
When my soda over topped.

Then suddenly it occurred to me,
That a Soda is a Pop.

Joseph C. Sorensen

Grandma's warning

Spooky is the theme for Poems this year
Lean in my child, there's nothing to fear
From this old grandma sitting next to you
As you look and notice something new.
"Why grandma" you say with youthful surprise.
"What are those lines around your eyes?"
Then I think with a sly fox grin
Has he seen the hairs upon my chin
Or the hair on my head all white and thin?
The spooky truth of passing days
Is how fast they pass into memories haze.
I'll scare you now as much as I can
With the ravages of times cruel hand.
How your butt will sag and your boobs will too,
Your skin will wrinkle an d you can't tie your shoe.
Up in the night to pee three times, every staircase, an impossible climb.
Your voice will warble, your throat will crack.
Prunes will become your favorite snack.
People will call you deary now.

Your back will bend and your shoulders will bow.
So beware all you young little things
Hold onto your youth and tightly cling
To the myth that you can cheat old time.
And harken now to my little rhyme.
All the serums, creams or Botox true,
Will not stop a child from turning to you and patting your cheek and saying with glee, "oh grandma what is this I see? A wrinkle, a roll, a new white hair,"
You ask why I warn you from this lawn chair.
Cause the theme this year is to scare you a bit
So take heed of my warning in this little writ
Old man time will come for you
Be scared if you like, but her is naught you can do.

Mary Mealing

Wolf

T'was not a night for fairy lights,
Nor stars that flicker in the sky.
Nights like this are never sung,
In any mother's lullaby.

Cold and dark, the moon was full,
But hid her face behind black clouds.
Not a single friendly star,
Could pierce those unrelenting shrouds.

And I had wandered from the road,
Lost my way and lost my stead.
I heard the wind, it moaned at me,
A warning that I could not heed.

I searched in vain to find the path,
A forest hut, perhaps a light.
But in the dark I lost myself,
Deeper in the woods and night.

There was no sound except the wind,
The wind and my own stumbling gait.
Perhaps, I thought, until the 'morn,
I should shelter here and wait.

Then as I sat I heard a sound,
A far off, distant, mournful howl.
A dog I thought, then with a laugh;
Just the hooting of an owl.

My tinder box and cloak were tied,
On my saddle long since gone.
I huddled there against the cold,
Wishing for an early dawn.

The thick dark clouds began to part,
The moonlight breaking through the trees,
Casting shadows, ghostly shapes,
That seemed to move and then to freeze.

Then I heard the sound again,
A wolf no doubt, and getting near.
Close enough to catch my scent!
Suddenly I shook with fear.

The terror I cannot explain,
I am a man not weak of heart.
Many foes and battles fought,
Fierce strong men have felt my dart.

My flintlock ready, charged with ball,
And good dry powder in the pan,
For reasons I cannot explain,
I fired not, I turned and ran.

Sheer terror carried me along.
Thorns and branches cut and tore.
I gasped for breath, my heart near burst,
I ran till I could run no more.

Then I heard it close behind,
That unearthly mournful howl.
I went to ground, I hid myself.
I stilled my breath, close by: a growl!

My pistol held in shaking hand,
I raised the muzzle, aim unsure.
I fired as the shadowed beast,
Pinned me to the forest floor!

I awoke at morning's light,
Soaked in blood, not all my own.
No sign of the hunting wolf,
The forest still, I was alone.

No memory has yet returned,
To answer; how did I survive?
Did my pistol wound the beast?
Why did it leave me yet alive?

My wounds have healed without a trace,
My strength returned my body sound.
Yet, there is a fever still,
I caught upon the cold wet ground:

One day each month as daylight comes,
I awake sweat soaked and cold,
With no memory of the night.
One day each month, when the moon is full.

John Sorensen

103

Mystic Memories

The young girl that I used to be
Is sometimes here and feels like
me.
Those if's and only's that I had
Were sometimes good and
sometimes bad.

My dreams, my wants, my every
whim
Drove my efforts to the brim.
Each important, each a need,
All thought was action oft' ill-
conceived.

As years have drifted floating by
Life's memories become a sigh.
My logic takes a break and runs
Through melancholy tales of
fun.

Now if I only could allow
For times elusiveness and how
The thoughts I'd keep and
succour still
Would crowd my mind and soul
to fill.

Then all of mystics memories
Would now be my entireties.
So would I even still exist
If every thought could not desist,

And every action I have taken
Left me burdened unmistaken?

Oh for respite I would plead
Mercy, grace and loss instead.
Could I please be left with
wisdom
And gain release from guilts
condition.

Would that God might intervene
So time's constraints might more
be seen.
On eagles wings I then could fly
And wonder bless me as I die.

Merna Mongelli

Chapter 10 – Undated and Family tales

Family reunions are only one time and place for the family to share poetry or tell stories.

I imagine endless piles of no-longer blank books now filled with our musings or artistic expression. There are handwritten notes tucked in a journal, post it notes in a drawer in my desk. The school notebooks full of poems written in the margins. Or those written and worked in a poetry workshop as we learn to improve upon our natural gifts … The urge to write and the ability to see the world from unique perspectives is an undeniable force.

Writing is not the only artistry in the family. Although several of us have published books written about Science Fiction, Fantasy, Business topics or Horror, we also have painters, musicians, craftsmen, and many other ways of expressing our poets' hearts.

This chapter contains poems and stories submitted outside of the reunion. These stories, in rhyme or prose, are read nearly every Christmas, or sometimes just because we want to share. A few have been published in a children's book but are included here with permission.

In the coming years, our family will continue to write. More children will be taught, not only to express their thoughts through writing, but to present in front of a crowd – the pre-K child, with mom or dad writing down the words for them and kneeling beside them for support. They learn the ability to speak their words, their ideas, in front of a crowd of 50 or more people before they learn to spell their own words. Thus, we continue the raising of the next generation of poets.

Christmas Eve

Christmas Eve for our family, was filled with tradition.
Christmas Eve was about Christ. It was a sacred celebration that had Dad (and later, John) reading the Christmas story from Luke 2: 1-20 and Matthew 2: 1, 2, 10, 11. We are musical, so we would sing the appropriate carol for the verse – Away in a Manger, Hark the Herald Angels Sing, and ending with Silent Night. We would dress up as the characters and got our kids to take most of the parts as the family grew: Baby Jesus was usually the newest baby or a doll until when there wasn't a baby that year. The baby would be put in the manger. Angels, 3 wise men, shepherds, and sometime the farm animals – everyone took part. We continued this tradition until Mom passed away. Each family traveling to Grandma's house, if we could, eventually adding Zoom participants, filling the house with shared worship.

Santa Lucia

From our Scandinavian heritage we also celebrate *Santa Lucia*.
Traditionally this holiday is celebrated on December 13th.

"St. Lucia's Day, festival of lights celebrated in Sweden, Norway, and the Swedish-speaking areas of Finland on December 13 in honor of the Italian Saint: St. Lucia (St. Lucy). One of the earliest Christian martyrs, St. Lucia was killed by the Romans in 304 CE because of her religious beliefs.

In Scandinavian countries each town elects its own St. Lucia. The festival begins with a procession led by the St. Lucia designee, who is followed by young girls dressed in white and wearing lighted wreaths on their heads and boys dressed in white pajama-like costume singing traditional songs. The festival marks the beginning of the Christmas season in Scandinavia, and it is meant to bring hope and light during the darkest time of the year.

Families observe St. Lucia's Day in their homes by having one of their daughters (traditionally the eldest) dress in white and serve coffee and baked goods, such as saffron bread (*lussekatter*) and ginger biscuits, to the other members of the family."

Gathered at Grandma's house, one of the oldest granddaughters dresses as St. Lucia. We tell the story and invite each family member to join the remembrance of Santa Lucia. Each person is presented with a Christmas treat or a present (most often Christmas crackers). We do it as part of our Christmas Eve celebration rather than on the 13th. Usually, Rhea reads the history of the celebration as the white gowned granddaughter, wreath (with unlit candles) on head, hands out treats.

But then it's time for more Christmas Eve fun. John would read "The Christmas Topper" and others would read their works, "Auntie and the Reindeer" was traditional, even when using Zoom to gather.

We would gather round a table or three and out would come the Rook cards or Phase 10 or Boggle. The food and fun lasting until midnight or so. Then hustling our kids out to the car, snuggled up to get home before Santa arrived.

Christmas morning was all about presents and pictures and visiting each other to see what Santa had brought.

In addition to the Reunion and Christmas, we had two other big family celebrations.

Grandma's Birthday
The first Saturday in October was the day to celebrate *Grandma's birthday.*
There was always a pinata when we were younger. But as that became difficult, we started playing "the Grandma Game." Mom would collect dollar store treasures all year round: wooden spoons, toys, games, hair clips, shampoo, pretty soaps, handmade hot pads, and puzzles. Others would show up with their stash of pencils, picture frames or nail polish. As we gathered round the living room, sometimes sitting two deep, the stash would get dumped into the middle. We passed a pie tin with two dice around and around –

everyone getting many tries. Get doubles and you can pick a prize. On the final round, once the stuff is gone, doubles will let you steal something from someone else. And if anyone didn't get a prize, they get to choose whatever they want from someone else. It's not yours, really, until the game is over.

The Grandma Game is touched on by some of our poems. But it is always a tradition, squeezed in between LDS Church conference sessions.

Easter

Easter was the other big day. Saturday always had an Easter Egg Hunt in the yard. We used to hide the eggs everyone had colored. But one year we lost one somewhere in the yard (we always kept count), we never did find it. We switched to plastic eggs with candy or coins in them.

When we were young it was always real eggs. After we had found our basket's full, we would celebrate by "Going Eastering." Going to the hill in Emery designated by our family as "the Easter Hill" or after that land was sold, just out to the desert. Racing our eggs down the hills. Destroying most of them. But they weren't really meant to eat. The few that survived were made into devilled eggs for Sunday's dinner.
The cards would come out on Sunday night, and we would play until late.

Every Sunday Evening

Sundays were always days of gathering. Every Sunday evening someone would be at Grandma's house - usually enough people to deal out a hand of Rook.

When mom passed away, many of us felt the loss most poignantly on the empty Sunday evening. Where do we meet up when someone is traveling through town? How do we stay connected?

The Family Reunion is the best option we found. And even though the Family Reunion has been passed to the next generation, Mom's sister and niece still come. The Grandkids from each family have designated a representative. Two families share the prep and the work every year, passing the torch onto the next group year over year. It is the place where we can still gather. Now, the Reunion is the destination for us to meet up. We also have a Siblings Chat thread where we share everything like news of a new grandbaby to the beautiful peonies that have bloomed.

From here down are the stories we read at holidays, poems from our Sisters' weekend, and a few of the poems and stories that have meant a lot in our lives.

Morgan Templar

The Christmas Topper

I'll know it when I see it,
Aunt Millie said to me,
As we sought the perfect topper,
for the perfect Christmas Tree.

I know that we will find it,
I can feel it in my bones,
She muttered to herself,
As once again we started home.

We had searched in every
discount,
And Five-And-Dime in town,
And I was getting weary,
Of driving her around.

We had looked in every china
shop,
Scoured every Mall.
We had gone to every Jewelers,
And every hawkers stall.

From early in the morning,
Until it was late and dark,
We looked at thousands of them,
But none quite hit the mark.

We saw stars by the hundreds,
And angels by the gross.
Dolls and bells and animals,
And wreaths made out of floss.

Some were red and some were
green,
Some were blue and some were
rose.
One looked like a pig,
With a light stuck in it's nose.

But Aunt Millie snubbed them
all,
Without a second glance.
Ceramic shop to drug store,
They never had a chance.

Then just as I had given up,
And resigned myself to fail,
We passed a little gift shop,
And Aunt Millie gave a yell.

For displayed in the window,
Lit by lights of red and green,
Was a topper like no other,
Topper we had seen.

It was a kind of angel,
With fuzzy plastic hair.
Its wings were made of netting,
And arched back with a flair.

With fruit tucked under one arm,
And a wreath around it's head,
Hanging from it's outstretched
hand,
Were bells tied on with thread.

It had a sparkling halo,
And a necklace made of chain.
It sat astride a reindeer,
And held a candy cane.

Now I admit that mine,
Is the innocence of youth,
But I thought the thing was ugly,
If you want to know the truth.

Aunt Millie on the other hand,
Was trembling with glee.
She rushed into the gift shop,
Asking no advice from me.

Her face lit up like tree lights,
As she waved to the man.
She could hardly say a word,
Just pointed with her hand.

The Shopkeeper came quickly,
A relieved look in his eye.
He gladly took her money.
I thought the price too high.

Aunt Millie clutched her treasure,
As she hurried to the street.
She held it like a baby,
As she settled in her seat.

Hurry, hurry, drive us Home"!
"This is perfect for our tree!"
Now I am not an expert,
But it seemed less so to me.

This year our tree *was* special,
It had a certain kind of flair.
The family had spent hours,
Decorating it with care.

The lights and bulbs were perfect,
As was every piece of floss,
Not one piece of tinsel,
Was placed by careless toss.

And as we viewed our effort,
Each one proud of his part,
We realized our tree,
Was indeed a work of art.

Then Auntie turned to Mother,
And said "Oh please my dear,
Let me get the topper,
For our Christmas tree this year."

That was how it started,
How it all began.
But I didn't think this topper,
Was in my mother's plan.

We arrived at our front door.
Auntie went in on the run.
"We found it! We found it!
Come quickly everyone!"

The family came running,
And gathered all around,
To watch us place the topper,
That we had bought in town.

112

Aunt Millie held it up,
For everyone to see.
Then I climbed on a chair,
And placed it on the tree.

It was the kind of moment,
That just hangs and lingers.
The only sound was brother,
Laughing through his fingers.

My mothers mouth was open,
She looked a little ill.
Sister clutched Mom's elbow,
And stood there very still.

We might have stayed forever,
In that awful frozen state,
But suddenly the tree,
Could no longer bare the weight.

It made a swishing sound,
Like the sweeping of a broom,
And toppled to the floor,
In the middle of the room.

Now, I guess I should have
caught it,
But I stood and watched it fall,
And the perfect Christmas
Topper,
Smashed itself against the wall.

John Sorensen

Heritage

When Little Orphant Annie
came to our house to stay
We laughed and cried and
wrangled and wiled the days
away.

When Annie brushed the crumbs
away and dusted hearth and
sweep
We never thought it odd that she
should earn her keep.

She baked the bread she made
the fire
And told her tales of witches ire
Close we sat in the blue blaze
light
As she spoke of the gobbl'uns
and gave us all a fright.

So when the naughty boy who
wouldn't say his prayers
Was sought in room and cubby
hole away upstairs,

We stared in awe and wonder
and kept anticipations shout
All waiting for that frightful end
she'd speak without a doubt.

Oh what a time that was when
all was sound and true
Assured by passions stories like
Little Boy Blue.

That we were brought up
different never seemed to bear

Not on the mournful sorrows of
distant livings care.

Then we all just seemed to drift
in futures head bow.
And where the sail would take
us, its surely brought us now.

To sit in bright and shining light
of all our spirits glow
A place of wondered merriment
like times of long ago.

O family, friends, oh parents
dear
With hope and love we bend our
ear.
And gladly give our hearts and
prayers
To greater moments unawares.

And now we sit round
Grandma's knee
Each one their treasures all to
see.
We've brought our own, our
thoughts to share,
And with our hearts our burdens
bear.

So like Belinda's favorite friend
Whose own great story had no
end.
We've chased our lions down
the stairs,
And end our days with lighter
cares.

Unknown

114

If I Were a Child

If I were a child
And once I was
I wouldn't worry so much
About Santa Claus

I would get up early
On Christmas Day
And run outside
In the snow to play

I'd find a snow bank
s all white and pure
Where no one had been
Not a soul before

I'd throw myself down
In the fresh fallen flakes
And make a snow angel
With my arms and my legs

Then carefully I would
Get back up again
And looking at my angel
I would think about Him

I know why angels
Came that night
It wasn't y to make
Shepherds quake with fright

Their hearts were so full
That first Christmas night
They couldn't be silent
And hide from sight

They had to run
And shout and sing!
Their Savior was born
Their God and King!

I wonder if I
Was one of them
Singing that first
Joyful hymn

Or maybe I just
Stood quietly by
And watched and prayed
I'm sure I cried

Yes I'd look at my angel
There in the snow
And try to remember
What I used to know

If I were a child
And once I was
I think more about Jesus
Than old Santa Claus

Rhea Cragun

The Christmas Mouse

Once upon a Christmas Eve
When Santa Clause was young,
A little mouse came creeping
Out where the socks were hung.

He scampered up the Christmas
tree
And nibbled at the berries,
He ate part of the popcorn string
He even ate the cherries.

He dashed into the kitchen
Where sat the Christmas cake
He gobbled all the raisins
But left the sugared dates.

And just when he was thinking
Perhaps he'd had his share
He spied the bag of licorice
That hung from grandpa's chair.

Now licorice is a favorite treat
Of all mice, old or young,
When he saw those luscious
morsels
He nearly bit his tongue.

He ran across the kitchen rug
To where the licorice sat
But just before he got there
Out jumped our big black cat.

Now Tommy George is a
mousing cat
And quite the savage beast
When he saw that little mouse,
he thought,
"Ah, here's my Christmas feast."

Round and round the Christmas
tree
The cat chased the mouse that
night
And tripping on the electric
cords
They somehow lit the lights.

Orbs of red and gold and green
Shown as bright as day
Tommy George sat staring
And the mouse, he crept quietly
away.

Rhea Cragun

Pete the Christmas Prairie Dog

It was a wintery day all covered
with fog
When I first saw him, the
Christmas Prairie Dog.
The days were short and nights
were lonesome.
It was late in the season and was
heading home.

Now I admit I was tired from
lack of sleep
And there was ice on the
window from the blowing sleet.
I turned a corner and my truck
lights glowed
On the long flowing prairie
where it had just snowed.

There on the snowbank he stood
in my lights
And I thought, surely I had
imagined the sight.
Dressed all in red from his head
to his toes
With pieces of holly for buttons
and bows.

He was a small rodent of the
prairie dog persuasion
And he carried a small wreath
and a Christmas invitation.
I slammed on the brakes and slid
to a stop in the snow
My heart was beating and my
hands were froze.

As I climbed down from the
truck still shaking a little
He ran up beside me with a
laugh and a giggle.
He spoke to me in a voice quite
tiny yet firm
And told me this story with a
joyful turn.

As Santa provides for humans
their presents and yule log
For the small creatures of the
world it's the Christmas Prairie
Dog.
So it was there in the high
Nebraska plain
That I first learned of him and
that Pete was his name.

Pet*e* told me his story as we
supped on some nog
How he had become the
Christmas Prairie Dog.
*O*ne terrible winter when Pete
was just a lad
In a freezing winter storm, Pete
lost his dad.

His dad had been gathering the
Christmas feast
When he was caught in an ice
storm - Winter's Beast.
Pete in his sorrow began to mope
and whine
When he noticed a red suite
hanging on the line.

He thought of his siblings, their sad empty hands
And all the small creatures throughout the land.
He came up with a plan he knew they would love
And he put on the suit, a hat and some gloves.

At first he hung Christmas wreaths on each door
But he knew in his heart there was more to this chore.
So he gathered up berries, nuts, thistles and nettles
And filled tiny stockings made from dandelion petals.

And, as Christmas Prairie Dogs had done before,
He put the stockings in logs by each little one's door.
And each little child of the small creature kind
Will sing carols of Pete the Prairie Dog at Christmas time.

It is no surprise that they all know his name
His father's gift had been just the same.
Pete's father had also been the gift giving one
For Pete was the Christmas Prairie Dog's son.

I asked Pete why he had come to me on that cold winter night
And he said he needed a ride, he had missed his flight.
The Christmas Prairie Dog doesn't have his own sleigh
He hitches a ride as Santa passes his way.

But his legs are quite short and though he ran with *all* his might
The reindeer were too fast and flew out of sight.
So I gave Pete a ride on the dash of my 18 wheel sleigh
As I was heading north with toys anyway.

And when *Christmas* comes with snow and with sleet
The little ones will start dreaming of the Prairie Dog treats.
On *Christmas* morning they will run for th*eir* logs
Full of treats and delights from the Christmas Prairie Dog.

Rhea and Robert Cragun

Auntie and the Reindeer

Auntie killed Rudolf yesterday
night,
Now Santa can't get his sleigh
into flight.

Auntie killed Rudolf, all
mangled and bent,
Now Santa can't answer the
letters we sent.

Auntie killed Rudolf, smashed
him flat,
Now Santa won't come cause
he's hoppin' mad.

Auntie, oh Auntie, where was
your mind?
You don't kill reindeer at
Christmas time!

Auntie killed Rudolf, t'other
reindeer stood by.
I told grandma not to let Auntie
drive.

Auntie Killed Rudolf with her
car - not fun!
Next time, Auntie, use a gun!

Dasher and Dancer are dead for
a reason,
We got them last year for
hunting season.

Auntie killed Rudolf, now she's
so sad,
Cause Santa put her on his list,
marked bad.

Auntie, oh Auntie, where was
your mind?
You don't kill reindeer at
Christmas time!

Auntie killed Rudolf, his nose
won't glow,
To light the way on the fresh
fallen snow.

Auntie killed Rudolf, that's the
end of the game,
Christmas will never seem quite
the same.

Auntie, oh Auntie, where was
your mind?
You don't kill reindeer at
Christmas time!

Rhea E Cragun

119

A Trip to Santa's Village

Not too many years ago I took a
little trip.
Way up to the North Pole to visit
Santa for a bit.

I drove up to Alaska, up to the
frozen regions.
Just a couple months before the
Christmas season.

I had hoped to see old Santa, that
jolliest of elves
Packing toys and presents and
filling all the shelves.

But…

Santa was not happy, he heaved
a heavy sigh,
"I promised all the children toys
and now it seems I lied."

"What ever could you mean,
Santa Claus?" I said.
"You always have toys for
Christmas, at least that's what
I've read."

Santa took me to his workshop.
He showed me all around.
But no matter where we went I
never heard a sound.

"Where are all the elves?" I
asked, "Is there some kind of
strike?"

"No," said Santa Claus, "The
problem's my brother Mike."

Santa sat me on a stool and
shared with me this tale
About when he was just a lad
and had some toys to sell.

It seems that Santa's family is
bigger than we thought.
He has an older brother Mike
and a baby sister, Dot.

When Santa was a little child he
liked Christmas quite a bit
But never had the money to buy
all those special gifts.

So, on one fateful winter day
Santa, all sad and blue,
Went to ask his brother Mike
what he thought he should do.

Now, Mike wasn't evil, he just
wasn't very nice.
He was the kinda kid who threw
snowballs made of ice.

Mike said, "I have a plan. Here
is what you should do:
Bring me all your special toys,
bring the new ones too."

"We'll wrap them up in paper
and add a piece of string.
On each package we'll put a
price to sell each special thing."

"And to help you out" his
brother said holding out his fist
"I'll lend you half a sixpence to
buy the paper with."

"And you can pay me back
someday from the profits that
you make
From all the toys you sell, But
not the ones you break."

Santa took the three pence
shaking on the deal.
He ran into the winter night
Kicking up his heels.

Santa bought his paper he
wrapped up all the toys
He took them out to sell to all
the girls and boys.

As he walked through the streets
his sack upon his back,
He passed the old town
orphanage; the shutters all were
black.

Behind one darkened shutter
shown a tiny light.
Peeking through the window,
Santa saw a sorry sight.

All around the nursery floor sat
the little kids.
Their only toys were canisters,
some without the lids.

Santa thought about his toys and
about the little tikes.
He thought about the three pence
he owed his brother Mike.

Now Mike had said, "You pay
me back from the profits that
you make
Only on the toys you sell and not
the ones you break."

So Santa took each toy and,
unwrapped it from its paper
And broke a corner off each little
tiny treasure

He wrapped back up each toy
and took off all the tags.
Then he put each of the presents
back into his bag.

Picking up his bundle he went
around the back
And found a sturdy ladder beside
some tiny tracks.

Now keep in mind, this was
olden days when everything was
new
And there was magic in the air
that could make your dreams
come true.

Santa climbed up on the roof and
over to the flu.
He took out all the presents. He
knew just what to do.

He dropped all of the packages
down into the fireplace.
He couldn't wait to see the
smiles on each little orphan's
face.

He turned in such a hurry that he
slipped upon the snow.
As he began to fall he cried,
"Oh, Ho, Ho, Ho, Ho!"

As he fell into the darkness with
this cry of dismay
He fell upon the buckboard of a
reindeer drawn sleigh.

Now remember that I told you
there was magic 'round there
And each tiny little reindeer took
off into the air.

Now, all of this was interesting
and I told Santa so.
But it didn't explain his brother
Mike or about this elf no show.

Then Santa reminded me of the
three pence Mike had lent.
Santa can't pay him back
because he didn't have a cent.

All these years Mike had held
that three pence over Santa's
head
But this year he got fed up and
took the elves instead.

All Mike wanted was the three
pence as was his due.
Then he would return the elves
to make presents for me and you.

So I emptied all my pockets and
I counted all my change.
I had a total sixpence and a
plastic diamond ring.

I counted out three pennies and
dropped them in Santa's glove.
I said, "this don't half pay you
for your kindness and your
love."

So, Santa got his elves back and
the halls rang with joy
And the sound of tiny hammers
making Christmas toys.

Now I'm heading south again.
I'm heading for the sun.
I'm looking forward to
Christmas and all the toys and
fun.

And I know there will be toys
because I saw the elves.
And I know there is a Santa
'cause I shook his hand myself.

Rhea E Cragun

The Christmas Rabbit

'Twas just after Christmas
(Before Valentine's)
The snow had stopped falling
The stocking were lined

On chairs by the chimney,
(or was it the flu?)
The children were sleeping,
Saint Nicholas, too

Had been there and gone.
Leaving gifts by the score,
When there came a small sniff
And a scratch at the door.

Then softly as snowfall
And Silent as night
A wee tiny rabbit
Hopped into sight.

He stirred not a whisker
But gazed round the room
Then twitching an ear,
He hopped to the broom.

There, close behind it,
Where the shadows were deep,
Was a little black hole,
Where the mice were asleep.

He filled up their stockings
With bread clubs and cheese,
For he knew that old Santa
Had forgot to fill these.

Then at last, just as sunrise
Crept over the sill,
He hopped out the door
And over the hill.

And how do I know
That the rabbit was there?
Well, I found his wee prints
Where he hid 'neath the chair.

E. Lynn Sorensen

Amilia's Firecrackers

A long time ago when life was young and so was I, I once had a firecracker. Just one, no more, but that was enough to invoke fear into my heart.

You see when I was a boy of 10 or 11, firecrackers were one hundred percent illegal. And, they weren't just "oh, don't worry, nobody cares about that law anyway," or "Just make sure an adult helps you lite that," no they were ILLEGAL. The kind of illegal that every cop in the County shows up when you fire one off. The kind where, if your Dad caught you with one you would get a good swat and would be grounded until you were 21. The kind of illegal that made your heart race with fear and excitement just to have knowledge of someone having one. And I had one.

I can't remember where I got it, or from whom I got it, but I kept it in my pocket and every now and then I would bring it out to show someone or to impress a girl or a potential friend. Many times the recipient of my showing would inquire if he or she could buy it from me. Many a dollar was offered for the hope of obtaining my one prize possession, but to no avail. I was not going to part with it so easily, because at some point I plan on setting it off. Somewhere secret, out of the way of ear shot of the Law or Parents.

My plans changed one day, however, when a large enough sum of money was offered to me for my firecracker. I believe it was for a whopping three dollars. Well I could not resist, so I sold it. I probably wouldn't have fired it off anyway, I was too scared.

Shortly after that others would come up to me asking if I had any more and if I would sell them some. Sadly I would say no, but that sometimes I visited my cousin in Wyoming, a magical land where firecrackers were legal, and maybe I would get more. This made me a local hero. Not bad for a fifth grader.

But sadly as most hero stories go, my fame was very short lived. As the rumors grew that I was selling firecrackers, one potential, or hopeful buyer, went to my house and asked my Dad if I had any more firecrackers for sell.

Well, that was end of me that day. Needless to say it was very difficult to convince my dad that I was not a "black market" firecracker dealer and that I happen to have had one that I had sold.

After my weeklong sentence I promised that I would never possess a firecracker again. And, for the most part I held up to that promise. There were maybe a few instances with a Cherry Bomb and a M80, but mostly I was good. After all I didn't want to be fugitive from the Law.

Now time has passed, a lot of time. Times and Laws have slowly changed over the years.

So, I was sitting in my Family Room watching a little TV, when my six-year-old Granddaughter came running into the house all happy and excited. It is true that she's always happy and excited, but this time she was extremely excited. She could not wait to show her Grandpa what she had.

She reached deep into her pockets and pulled out three large bricks of non-other than, you guessed it, "firecrackers." She had the biggest smile on her face and was begging me to go outside and lite them off.

I thought about how different things are and I just started to laugh. My little Granddaughter had her hands full of firecrackers, something I could have gone to jail for at one point, but now it was a Grandpa Granddaughter bonding moment. My how times had changed, and it made me laugh even harder. And somewhere from behind me, I don't know where, I could hear my Dad laughing as hard as I was.

I gave my little Amilia a great big hug and we headed off outside to fire off those little baby sticks of dynamite.

I still have some of those firecrackers in my dresser drawer, and to this day every time I see them, I smile and laugh.

Joseph C. Sorensen

125

The Three Gardens of the Plan of Happiness
(Inspired by "The Purifying Power of Gethsemane" By Elder Bruce R. McConkie, 1985)

The Garden of Eden

In a garden green and filled with life
A single voice is heard
"Now let us bring to all mankind
The glory of the earth"

"Let trees of every fruit abound
And creatures of all kind
And let the man and woman roam
Its secret to unwind"

The start of it was in a garden
No beams and so no motes
The start of it was in Paradise
No struggle and so no growth

"What's this you say, what's this?"
A tree we dare not eat
Or death will then be measured out.
"Not death, but you'll be free."

"I know thee now, oh serpent old
Thy lies have led me in"
But better to know good from bad
And the sorrow for our sin

Flee the garden's alluring scent
Now closed and left behind
Better for sorrow, grief and pain
Now faith and hope intwine

Struggles strengthen, errors teach
Lessons of God's true care and love
A Savior to atone for grief and sin
To Provide the path to home above

The Garden of Gethsemane

Oh, retched man, oh man of grief
Acquainted with much sorrow
To a garden wall on hands and knees
No Balm of Gilead to borrow

In this garden of ancient trees
In this grove of healing oils
Upon his shoulders he holds the world
With all its pain and human foils

Friends abandon him in sleep
An angel bodes him up
"Father if it be thy will,
I will drink the bitter cup"

In a garden with cool morning breeze
A betrayer plants a kiss
The tree bows shudder in the wind

126

The rabble raise their angry fists

Death! A sigh, the whole world
sighs
A God has died, a God has died!

Darkness falls and the earth is
shattered
With lightning strikes and
thunder
The mountain burst, the people
flee
The veil is torn asunder

The Garden tomb
There's a quiet place in the
garden
Of meditation and of peace
A cool cave in the back by the
wall
Where tired bones can sleep

Bring him here the owner pleads
Rest his head upon my shelf
A borrowed tomb but gently
laid
With spices of greatest wealth

Three Mary's and one Salome
Mourners and dear friends
In sorrow they prepare the herbs
Then wait for sabbath end

To the garden wall and to the
tomb
She comes early while others
sleep
Oh, Who will move the stone for
her

Who will comfort as she weeps?

What? The stone is rolled,
The Master's body gone from
the place
In sorrow She falls to the ground
The empty tomb she cannot face

"Oh gardener, if thou hast taken
him
Please let me take him hence,
Let me bear his body here away
To some other garden fence"

"Mary" the Master's voice
Her eyes they now can see
"Mary my beloved one"
She falls weeping at his feet

Alive! The Great I Am is risen!
Alive! And death has no sting!
From a garden tomb to his
Father's house
To all, He alone, salvation brings

He met the match and drank the
cup
Has drank for us the gall
Rejoice, rejoice, such love as
this
To save us from the fall.

The Savior of mankind is come
To save us from our sins
Oh, praise the plan of happiness
Oh shout, you world, "Amen!"

Rhea Cragun

127

Poems from: *Always Sisters – 2023 Capital Reef*

Canyon Trail

I feel the day is waning
As I trudge along through time
I lift my eyes and wonder
Who's at the forefront of this
line?

The pace is quickening
gradually
No time for second guessing
Is there ample time I ask myself
To walk the opposite direction?

My purpose lost
I slow my pace
The sun still warm upon my
face

My thoughts return to calm
I sit myself upon the trail
And accepting, await the dawn.

Susan L. Sorensen

Insect

Soul of air and water
An entity pictoral
Live in swamp and pool
Literally littoral

Pinned to film by canvas
Life and death combining
Air and water ended
The soul continues shining

From egg to pupae grown
The future all unknown

Awaits the gentle flyer
A thing of curiosity
Forever held in stasis
Becomes a mere monstrosity.

E. Lynn Sorensen

Shadow

A shadow on the rock
Ahead of what is there
Recall, flew, fly
Or overcome the fear

Flying fast across the sky
A shape on red slick rock
Is it Vulture, Owl, or gull
Or another Red Tail Hawk?

A screech, a movement, an
attack
The same movement coming
back
A flutter of wings in mirror
motion
A recognition of self appears
A chance to find acceptance
And dispel the first thought of
fear.

Mary Mealing

129

Lessons

I rode through dark upon my
steed
And all around me shook
The light shot forth above my
head
And all my breath was took

No quiet night, this deepening
plane
Yet soundless in its cry
No noise above the shadows lost
As light takes on the sky

Be still my steed, no fears to
form
The night will end and bring the
morn

And once again as two we ride
In nature's heaven, our sweet
earth
And take our lessons as they
come
Each one reflections of its worth.

Merna Mongelli

Miracles

In darkness search for sunshine
Frightened, scared and lost
Running from the fear of past
The future found, but at such
cost

Stepping past the tumbled walls
Into the empty fields
Walking into the unknown light
The sword of hope she yields

Awash with hope empirical
She asks, "Where are the
Miracles?"

Gaining strength from memory
 Moving forward now with calm
Miracles come after loss
Strength comes after alms.

Rhea Cragun

130

Driftwood in the Desert

Time captured in swirling
morass
Light, dark, movement swells
Is it wood, stone, or mud
Forever captured, writhing in
perils

Current flowing, creating a
memory
Wood growing to elements meet
Strain, grain forced to work
To provide armor to grain,
strong and sweet

A moment caught made timeless
again
Healed wounds of weather or
pain

A lesson we can carry
Life and strain will shape us
Strength grows with pressure
Accept and grow and become
thus

Morgan Templar

Escalante Canyon Art Festival

I come from home to this desert
place
To open my life to an artist
space
To workshops and demos and
friends anew
To marvel at talent and their
fresh point of view

The makers and bakers and poet
picture takers
At weeks end
Have new friends

I'll mark my calendar for next
year's fun
A time to camp in the desert sun
Now back to Heber for the
winter's start
And a chance to do some pastel
art

Thanks Lisa and Escalante town
For hosting us all and showing
us around
To make art in this special place
Is my favorite thing and puts a
smile on my face.

Mary Mealing

Negative Space and Dark Matter

Look between the leaves and
branches
Think of open space, then pass
into the vastness

Negative space and dark matter
Hold the universe in place
But often are dismissed
As negligible and waste

But, without there is no light;
Without there is no use
And color cannot perch
On a canvas without tooth.

Rhea Cragun

General Merchandise

In this earthly exchange of
living, giving,
Taking and sharing
The human commodity: loving
Hating, holding, caring,
Our earnest expenditure of
capital;
Saving, spending, reinvesting –
In this people's exchange
Of heavenly increase, life
divesting,
We are all General Merchandise.

E. Lynn Sorensen

People's Exchange Gen. MDSE.

Plain red brick
House of another age.
Will I find a family home?
A store for things I need?
Or will I see faces for sale
Stolen from lives and family
For profit and greed.

Morgan Templar

Art on the Run

Beauty held in light and shade
Painted rocks that inspire
Subject immobile dances and
changes
As the sun's rays move and play
With heat and radiance
Shadow and fire

Artists forced to hike to see it
Carrying it back for us to
treasure.

Morgan Templar

132

Food Truck

What impetus led you and yours
To steel your will and leave
behind
The streets and smells of
childhood play
For the land you've come to
know?

The dreams you carried in your
heart
Became the business that you've
grown
Do you bring your home into the
food
Or is it the food that takes you
home?

Susan Sorensen

My dog no more

Lonely, Lost, so ill-conceived
leaves me to wonder.

That this one small being
changed all that was broken.

Never before and never will be
again. This walk so alone.

How could I have known a loss
so great, when my cup was
always full.

Merna Mongelli

Girl in White

She walked forward through our
space
Her face a visage, to all offers
grace.

A smile for her, Lifting him up,
The world made beautiful by her
proffered cup.

Her story known, grace we see
Always offering love, lifting
those around me.

We see her dressed in white,
quite stark
The world she sees is burned and
dark.

Morgan Templar

Striped, bright beach towels

Flags proclaiming allegiance
To summer dalliance
Fluttering to natures music
Last frenetic celebration

Christine Seegmiller

Poems from our Childhood

Little Orphant Annie

Little Orphant Annie's come to
our house to stay,
An' wash the cups an' saucers
up, an' brush the crumbs away,
An' shoo the chickens off the
porch, an' dust the hearth, an'
sweep,
An' make the fire, an' bake the
bread, an' earn her board-an'-
keep;
An' all us other childern, when
the supper things is done,
We set around the kitchen fire
an' has the mostest fun
A-list'nin' to the witch-tales 'at
Annie tells about,
An' the Gobble-uns 'at gits you
    Ef you
      Don't
        Watch
          Out!

Onc't they was a little boy
wouldn't say his prayers,—
So when he went to bed at night,
away up stairs,
His Mammy heerd him holler,
an' his Daddy heerd him bawl,
An' when they turn't the kivvers
down, he wasn't there at all!
An' they seeked him in the
rafter-room, an' cubby-hole, an'
press,

An' seeked him up the chimbly-
flue, an' ever'wheres, I guess;
But all they ever found was thist
his pants an' roundabout--
An' the Gobble-uns'll git you
    Ef you
      Don't
        Watch
          Out!

An' one time a little girl 'ud
allus laugh an' grin,
An' make fun of ever'one, an'
all her blood an' kin;
An' onc't, when they was
"company," an' ole folks was
there,
She mocked 'em an' shocked
'em, an' said she didn't care!
An' thist as she kicked her heels,
an' turn't to run an' hide,
They was two great big Black
Things a-standin' by her side,
An' they snatched her through
the ceilin' 'fore she knowed
what she's about!
An' the Gobble-uns'll git you
    Ef you
      Don't
        Watch
          Out!

An' little Orphant Annie says
when the blaze is blue,
An' the lamp-wick sputters, an'
the wind goes *woo-oo*!
An' you hear the crickets quit,
an' the moon is gray,
An' the lightnin'-bugs in dew is
all squenched away,--
You better mind yer parents, an'
yer teachers fond an' dear,
An' churish them 'at loves you,
an' dry the orphant's tear,
An' he'p the pore an' needy ones
'at clusters all about,
Er the Gobble-uns'll git you
      Ef you
        Don't
          Watch
          Out!

James Whitcomb Riley

The Tale of Custard the Dragon

Belinda lived in a little white house, With a little black kitten and a little grey mouse, And a little yellow dog and a little red wagon, And a realio, trulio, little pet dragon.

Now the name of the little black kitten was Ink, And the little grey mouse, she called her Blink, And the little yellow dog was sharp as Mustard, But the dragon was a coward, and she called him Custard.

Custard the dragon had big sharp teeth, And spikes on top of him and scales underneath, Mouth like a fireplace, chimney for a nose, And realio, trulio, daggers on his toes.

Belinda was as brave as a barrel full of bears, And Ink and Blink chased lions down the stairs, Mustard was as brave as a tiger in a rage, But Custard cried for a nice safe cage.

Belinda tickled him, she tickled him unmerciful, Ink, Blink and Mustard, they rudely called him Percival, They all sat laughing in the little red wagon At the realio, trulio, cowardly dragon.

Belinda giggled till she shook the house, And Blink said Week!, which is giggling for a mouse, Ink and Mustard rudely asked his age, When Custard cried for a nice safe cage.

Suddenly, suddenly they heard a nasty sound, And Mustard growled, and they all looked around. Meowch! cried Ink, and Ooh! cried Belinda, For there was a pirate, climbing in the winda.

Pistol in his left hand, pistol in his right, And he held in his teeth a cutlass bright, His beard was black, one leg was wood; It was clear that the pirate meant no good.

Belinda paled, and she cried, Help! Help! But Mustard fled with a terrified yelp, Ink trickled down to the bottom of the household, And little mouse Blink strategically mouseholed.

But up jumped Custard, snorting like an engine, Clashed his tail like irons in a dungeon, With a clatter and a clank and a jangling squirm He went at the pirate like a robin at a worm.

The pirate gaped at Belinda's dragon, And gulped some grog from his pocket flagon, He fired two bullets but they didn't hit, And Custard gobbled him, every bit.

Belinda embraced him, Mustard licked him, No one mourned for his pirate victim Ink and Blink in glee did gyrate Around the dragon that ate the pyrate.

Belinda still lives in her little white house, With her little black kitten and her little grey mouse, And her little yellow dog and her little red wagon, And her realio, trulio, little pet dragon.

Belinda is as brave as a barrel full of bears, And Ink and Blink chase lions down the stairs, Mustard is as brave as a tiger in a rage, But Custard keeps crying for a nice safe cage.

Ogden Nash

Old Hyope

Dear old Hyope who was once so alive and gay,

Now he has his own little corner where he must stay.

Because of laws he is tied to a stake

Around and around he goes from morning to night

Starting his pace at the coming light.

For exercise he has worn a hard trail around a little lake.

Often he looks in his pan to see

If perhaps some scraps or cool water might be.

Are his old eyes bright or are they dim,

Does he see the tall sunflowers surrounding him?

Often when the sun shines hot does he wish for some clouds to come

To shut out the burning rays of the sun?

A cozy little house has been built for him.

Which to him is a blessing when winter sets in.

Do you children say, "Hi Hyope" give him a pat or a kind word or two

To let him know he is still one of you?

Time was when old Hyope was a glossy young pup

Back in Emery when the children were growing up.

Then he was as free as the children and could go where he pleased,

Climbing hills and wading in streams.

An d he didn't seem to mind a little switch

When he trampled down flowers while playing catch.

Then he could find a cool place to lie down and stretch.

He was a joy to the family when he was able to play,

But that was way back in his yesterday.

Now he is grey, shabby and old,

But his love for the children has never grown cold.

Most of them have grown up;

And have other affairs to keep up,

Oft times they unleash him but hold to the chain.

His joy is boundless because he is free again.

And he knows for sure he is still one of them.

Tho this heart seems strong,

We know by his age we won't have him long.

Sometime in winter when the frost is all about,

He will stay in his house and refuse to come out.

We know then he won't be with us much longer, we hope;

They will find a quiet resting place for dear old Hyope.

Myrtle Sorensen
(Birdell's mother)

Poem To My Nurse

Please look at me nurse, what do you ?
What do you think when you're looking at me?
A crabby old woman and not very wise,
Uncertain of habit with far away eyes?
Who dribbles her food and makes no reply
When you say to her, "I do wish you'd try."
Who seem not to notice the things that you do.
And forever is losing a stocking or shoe.
Is that what you're thinking; is that what you see?
The open your eyes nurse, you're not looking at me.

I was a small child with father and mother,
a sister and brothers who loved one another.
A sweet young girl with wings on her feet
And dreaming of a man that some day she'd meet.
Then a bride and a mother with young of my own
And a husband to build a secure happy home.
Now dark days are upon me, my husband is dead,
As I look to the future I shudder with dread.
I remember my children with young of their own,
And I think of all the sweet love I have known.

I'm just an old woman and nature is cruel
Sometimes I do think that I look like a fool.
But inside this old carcass a young girl still dwells,
And when I think of it all my battered heart swells.
I remember the joy, I remember the pain, as I think of my life, again and again.
I think of the years all too few, gone so fast,
And accept the reality that nothing can last.
So open your eyes nurse, open and see. Not a crabby old woman. Look closer, see me.

Myrtle Sorensen
(Birdell's mother)

These two poems were written by Myrtle Sorensen, Birdell Sorensen's mother, enclosed in a letter sent to Elva and Birdell while she was residing in the nursing home in Ferron.

140

Other Published Works by the Family:

Morgan Templar
Get Governed: Building World Class Data Governance Programs.
Ivory Lady Publishing, September 13, 2017
A Culture of Governance. Ivory Lady Publishing, August 31, 2018

David Mealing
Soul of the World (The Ascension Cycle, Book 1). Orbit Publishing,
June 27, 2017
Blood of the Gods (The Ascension Cycle, Book 2). Orbit
Publishing, August 21, 2018
Chains of the Earth (The Ascension Cycle, Book 3). Orbit
Publishing, December 12, 2023

Joshua P. Sorensen
Picture Books
Old MacGregor's Farm. War Monkey Publications, LLC. 1 December 2021.
What Scared Caesar. War Monkey Publications, LLC. 1 August 2019.
Zombies Just Love People. War Monkey Publications, LLC. 16 May 2018.
Short Stories
"Trick-Or-Treat". I Used to be an Animal Lover. D.A. Cairns. May 1, 2023.
"Sour". Dead Stars and Stone Arches. Timber Ghost Press. June 15, 2022.
"The Au Pair". The Witching Time of Night. Salt City Genre Writers.
October 1, 2020.
"Hunting Season". From The Yonder, Volume I. War Monkey Publications,
LLC. June 1, 2020.
"NORAD". Peaks of Madness: A Collection of Utah Horror. Forty-Two
Books. April 1, 2019.
"The Sign". Peaks of Madness: A Collection of Utah Horror. Forty-Two
Books. April 1, 2019.
"A Little Night Visit". The Hunger: A Collection of Utah Horror. Twisted
Tree Press. April 10, 2018.
"Mouthwash". The Hunger: A Collection of Utah Horror. Twisted Tree
Press. April 10, 2018.

Poetry
"Three Naughty Goats". The Big Book of Things That Go Bump in the

Dark. Timber Ghost Press. 2023.

"Why Are Children So Delicious?". Wasatch Witches. Fear Knocks Press. March 15, 2021.

"Two Candles". Inspired, Vol. 6. Rock Canyon Poets, November 2020.

"Tailgater". Inspired, Vol. 6. Rock Canyon Poets, November 2020.

"Simian Thoughts". Inspired, Vol. 6. Rock Canyon Poets, November 2020.

"Fog". The Handy, Uncapped Pen, 2020.
http://www.handyuncappedpen.com/2020/08/fog-by-joshua-p-sorensen.html

"Your iPhone iHates You". Inspired, Vol. 5. Rock Canyon Poets, November 2019.

"Florida Gator". Inspired, Vol. 5. Rock Canyon Poets, November 2019.

"Lonely Notes". Inspired, Vol. 5. Rock Canyon Poets, November 2019.

"Less Traveled By". Peaks of Madness: A Collection of Utah Horror. Forty-Two Books. April 1, 2019.

"Respite of Thought". Peaks of Madness: A Collection of Utah Horror. Forty-Two Books. April 1, 2019.

"Gourmand". Peaks of Madness: A Collection of Utah Horror. Forty-Two Books. April 1, 2019.

"To the Doubters". Inspired, Vol. 4. Rock Canyon Poets, November 2018.

"Procter & Gamble". Inspired, Vol. 4. Rock Canyon Poets, November 2018.

"Monster's Feast". The Hunger: A Collection of Utah Horror. Twisted Tree Press. April 10, 2018.

"Harpy". The Hunger: A Collection of Utah Horror. Twisted Tree Press. April 10, 2018.

"Reveried Orc-Dream". Sibyl's Scriptorium, Vol. 5. Sibyl's Scriptorium Inc. 2018.

"Hail Mary". Inspired, Vol. 3. Rock Canyon Poets, November 2017.

"JAZZ". Inspired, Vol. 3. Rock Canyon Poets, November 2017.

"Orchestra". Inspired, Vol. 3. Rock Canyon Poets, November 2017.

"Mariner's Prayer". Sibyl's Scriptorium, Vol. 4. Sibyl's Scriptorium Inc, 2017.

"Wasted Memories". Inspired, Vol. 2. Rock Canyon Poets, November 2016.

"Stickball in the Orchard". Inspired, Vol. 2. Rock Canyon Poets, November 2016.

"Plague Limericks and Rhymes". "World Horror Convention 2016 Program Guide", April 28, 2016.

Expected Publications: (Accepted for Publication in 2024)

"My Undead Neighbor". Lost Between Light and Shadow. Carlisle Legacy Books, LLC. 2024.

"Penpals". Lost Between Light and Shadow. Carlisle Legacy Books, LLC. 2024.

"The Ghost of My Room". Lost Between Light and Shadow. Carlisle Legacy Books, LLC. 2024.

Skye Caden
Short Stories
"Kla-Rump Went The Staircase". <u>Sibyl's Scriptorium, Vol. 4</u>. Sibyl's Scriptorium Inc, 2017.

Poetry
"Mafia Man". <u>Inspired, Vol. 3</u>. Rock Canyon Poets, November 2017.
"Learn To Label". <u>Sibyl's Scriptorium, Vol. 4</u>. Sibyl's Scriptorium Inc, 2017.
"Time Loop". <u>Inspired, Vol. 2</u>. Rock Canyon Poets, November 2016.
"Paranoid". <u>Poetry Showcase, Vol.3</u>. Horror Writers Association, August 7, 2016.
"There Can't Possibly Be A Ghost Here". "World Horror Convention 2016 Program Guide", April 28, 2016.

Expected Publications: (Accepted for Publication in 2024)
"House of the Fun Dead". <u>Lost Between Light and Shadow</u>. Carlisle Legacy Books, LLC. 2024

Brian Mealing
Short Stories
"Tasty Good". <u>The Big Book of Things That Go Bump in the Dark</u>. Timber Ghost Press. 2023.

Poetry
"I Have". <u>Inspired, Vol. 6</u>. Rock Canyon Poets, November 2020.
"Snakes". <u>Peaks of Madness: A Collection of Utah Horror</u>. Forty-Two Books. April 1, 2019.
"Fully-charged". <u>Inspired, Vol. 3</u>. Rock Canyon Poets, November 2017.

Expected Publications: (Accepted for Publication in 2024).
"Devour Like Sharks". <u>Lost Between Light and Shadow</u>. Carlisle Legacy Books, LLC. 2024
"Mermaids". <u>Lost Between Light and Shadow</u>. Carlisle Legacy Books, LLC. 2024.

E. Lynn Sorensen
Poetry

"Say My Name". <u>Inspired, Vol. 6</u>. Rock Canyon Poets, November 2020.

"Erratics". <u>Inspired, Vol. 6</u>. Rock Canyon Poets, November 2020.

"I am Leaf". <u>Inspired, Vol. 5</u>. Rock Canyon Poets, November 2019.

"Lonely Little World". <u>Inspired, Vol. 5</u>. Rock Canyon Poets, November 2019.

"Hand Woven". <u>Inspired, Vol. 4</u>. Rock Canyon Poets, November 2018.

"Bird by Bird". <u>Inspired, Vol. 4</u>. Rock Canyon Poets, November 2018.

"Strange Lands". <u>Inspired, Vol. 3</u>. Rock Canyon Poets, November 2017.

"In The Fall". <u>Inspired, Vol. 3</u>. Rock Canyon Poets, November 2017.

"Ghost Story". <u>Inspired, Vol. 3</u>. Rock Canyon Poets, November 2017.

www.ingramcontent.com/pod-product-compliance
Lightning Source LLC
Chambersburg PA
CBHW050947030426
42339CB00007B/317